THE TOMMIE SCOTT STORY

FROM GANGS, DRUGS, AND CRIME TO SOLDIER FOR CHRIST

TOMMIE SCOTT

To my eternal Brother Mark I love you Keep the Fire burning

Eph 7:2

innovo
PUBLISHING

Published by
Innovo Publishing, LLC
www.innovopublishing.com
1-888-546-2111

Providing Full-Service Publishing Services for
Christian Authors, Artists & Organizations: Hardbacks, Paperbacks,
eBooks, Audiobooks, Music & Videos

THE TOMMIE SCOTT STORY

Unless otherwise noted, Scripture is taken from The Official King James Bible Online,
Authorized Version (KJV), kingjamesbibleonline.org. Bible Gateway,
New King James Version, biblegateway.com

Library of Congress Control Number: 2013916685
ISBN 13: 978-1-61314-165-6

Cover Design & Interior Layout: Innovo Publishing, LLC

Printed in the United States of America
U.S. Printing History

First Edition: December 2013

DEDICATION

I dedicate my life story to all of the people who tried to help me avoid the path of destruction that almost took my life. At the top of my list are my mom and my lovely wife. Throughout all my trials, they showed me unconditional love and never gave up on me. In addition, there were teachers, counselors, coaches, inmates, and others who sought to direct me to God.

FOREWORD

I have been involved in prison and jail ministry, as well as crisis intervention ministry with Centrum of Hollywood and Centrum of Las Vegas for forty years. I was also casting director on the feature film *The Cross and the Switchblade*. This movie tells the story of gang leader Nicky Cruz and has impacted tens of thousands of lives worldwide. Tommie's story has the same potential to bring hope and show the way out of destructive lifestyles. *The Tommie Scott Story* is a story for kids to help them avoid gangs and drugs. It is also a story of hope for everyone who needs a miracle. Tommie's story should be placed in every juvenile and adult correctional facility.

Kleg Seth

TABLE OF CONTENTS

PREFACE

We live in a world that says the hope for the future is in money, possessions, and power. This creates the illusion in our society that life is all about *me*, what *I* can get, and *my* well-being only. Disappointment and rejection often lead to resentment and a "forget everybody else" attitude. After all, this is human nature in a world of fallen people who will soon pass away, right? My story is a story of hope—a hope that endures forever.

I wrote this story to give a message of HOPE and show how you can have peace, regardless of the evil in this world. It is tragic that each year the United States has approximately 15,000–16,000 murders, 2–3 million other violent crimes, 80,000–100,000 rapes, along with an additional 6 million crimes like burglary, grand larceny, car theft, extortion, white-collar crimes, etc.[1] If you do the math, you won't be able to sleep at night. It is worse in many other countries of the world, and these stats are swept under the rug. So please help me spread hope so lives can be saved.

---

[1] The Disaster Center, www.disastercenter.com/crime/uscrime.htm

Chapter One

WHERE IT ALL BEGAN

I was born March 15, 1980, in Los Angeles, California. We called LA "killer Cali." I was the son of Tommie and Dana and brother to my two sisters, Tasha and Tanya. I was a quiet kid who didn't usually show people my feelings. As a young kid, my heart was still in its sweet, gentle state. I loved animals. I was a typical boy who put bugs in my pocket and enjoyed the numbness and taste that came from putting an ant on my tongue.

I was five years old when my mom and dad divorced. Preceding the divorce, our home was a whirlwind of fights and arguments between my mom and dad. Even today, I remember hitting my dad with my toy fire truck when they fought. My dad was violent and abusive to my mother, and I remember those traumatic events; they'll stick with me for life. It's amazing how much I remember from when I was five. I remember how scared I was for my mom and me. But growing up, I never talked about it.

The fighting and abuse ended when my mother left the house with my sisters and me and filed for a divorce. She, unlike many unfortunate wives in the same circumstance, was able to run and not look back.

The divorce forced my dad to provide for his family, so even though he was in and out of prison, his focus was on taking care of us financially. Unfortunately, the money wasn't enough. He neglected to actually spend time with us, and spending time with his dad is what every young boy looks forward to more than anything.

My mom, my sisters, and I ended up going to a shelter to live until my mother could figure out what to do next. We didn't have the money to move into a new place right away; the shelter was our only option. It wasn't too bad as a young kid. We had a playground, some new (used) clothes they gave us, a room, and food. I imagine this must have been very stressful for my mom.

After several months, Mom took us kids with her to move in with my grandmother in her single-bedroom apartment until our Section 8 papers came, then we moved to some housing projects in a neighboring city. We had very little food to eat and no furniture to sit on. My mom was a genius with food. Our first meal was a mayo sandwich—just mayo and bread. I thought it was the best sandwich ever; it was like the sandwich fell straight from heaven. Then out of nowhere, she brought in a milk crate for us to use as a couch. My mom was the best at creative improvising.

For a very long time, my mom would not even look at another man. She didn't trust them. We never saw her flirting or even any sign of interest at all. But after what she went through, she still had joy. She was always happy, silly, and outgoing. We always went to the beach and the movies. My mom could name every actor in the business at that time. I had a fun mom. She would cry if she had to yell at us or give us a whooping. She would also cry if she couldn't pay the bills. My sisters and I would catch her from time to time crying in her room. I guess she left her problems in the room because when she came out, she was silly again. I know my mom had a lot of worries and stress, but no matter what, she made sure we felt love.

ELEMENTARY SCHOOL

We started elementary school at Catskill Avenue Elementary School. My sisters and I had our brand-new Pro Wings on with our secondhand clothes. In our eyes, we felt like little movie stars; we were what we called Cali fresh.

The first four years were the good years; it was about the fifth year when things started to go downhill for me. Reality at this early age hit me pretty hard. The absence of my father and the thoughts of him in another relationship and having other kids struck a nerve in me. These ill feelings began to fester and pretty soon, trouble followed me in school.

I didn't like being told what to do, and I didn't listen. I didn't want to try my best because my teachers weren't my parents, and my parents were the only ones I felt had the right to tell me what to do. At least that's what I told myself. I would steal from my teachers when they weren't looking. My fourth-grade teacher, who wore big glasses and had a strange voice, really irritated me. In retrospect, I can see that she really liked me and that's why she was so hard on me. I think she could see my potential. But I would still throw paper balls at her, and one time, I even broke a pencil in two and threw it at her when she turned her back to write on the chalkboard. This was just the beginning of my rebellion against authority. A lot of trouble followed.

FAMILY

With my dad out of the picture most of the time, I had no father figure or positive male role model in my life. My dad was constantly in and out of jail. He was never at any of my tee-ball games or any other sports event so I got applause from my mom and other kids' dads. This had a major impact on who I had started to become. As I look back, I see that even with a great mom I began disliking myself more and more. I felt worthless. I felt like a good-for-nothing little boy.

When he was out of jail, my dad did take care of my entire family, including cousins and aunts. Perhaps in his own way, my dad did care for us. He even took care of his friends, the ones he grew up with who were strung out on cocaine. He would hire them for various jobs around the house and even give them shelter and food. He never gave up on his family or friends. But his downfall was his addiction to the streets and the way he chose to provide for his family, which was the only way he knew—hustling. With six other kids besides us and having no education but the streets, he had to make money and make it fast. This was all during a time when racial tensions were flaring in Los Angeles.

Blacks started to develop neighborhood protection groups to watch over their communities. When the Bloods and Crips were born, my dad was one of the first Crips in the country. He was part of the 103rd St. Grape Street Watts Crips. They call him Big Tommie today, but back in the day, they called him something else. His big brother, my uncle Bud, was from PJ Watts Crips. These were two of the most notorious Crip gangs, maybe the worst in the country.

In 1948, my granny Woe moved to Los Angeles, California, from Shreveport, Louisiana, at the age of sixteen with her mother, Manntie Bell James. Why, I don't know. In 1951, she had her first child, my uncle Bud, while living in the Imperial Courts Housing Project in Watts. After Uncle Bud, came my aunt Barbra Jean, Aunt Debra, Aunt Joyce, Uncle David, and then my dad.

My dad didn't know his father. He ran the streets of Watts and committed crimes that introduced him to the juvenile system early on. He escaped from the juvenile jail Camp Glen Rocky where I was to end up later on.

My granny Woe's house was the place that our entire family, even those we hadn't seen for a while, would meet up for the holidays. I looked forward to the time I got to spend with my sisters, cousins, aunts, and for a while, my uncle David. He was the middle brother who later passed away from cancer. My uncle Bud, my dad's oldest brother, had gotten his life together after a long drug rehabilitation. He went on to teach at UCLA. Eventually, he went back to using heroin and contracted AIDS from sharing needles. He later passed away from the virus.

Granny's place was full of love and joy. She was always laughing and loved having us sit on her lap as she gave us big, wet kisses. One day when I was playing in her driveway, there was a big puddle of oil on the ground. When we played, Granny always came out to see if we were messing up her garden or her neighbor's garden. With her country accent she would say, "Tummy (Tommie), don't you step in that earl (oil) now." We would nearly lose our breath from laughing so hard. Her accent got us every time.

When my aunt Debra drank, we could easily get her to give us money. All we would have to say was, "Auntie, can I have some money for the ice-cream truck?" BAM! A ten-dollar bill. In those days, ten dollars was like a hundred.

Aunt Joyce, the middle sister, was stricter. I liked her but I think she was misunderstood. I thought she had her stuff together, but others might have disagreed. Her daughters, Taronda and Ladona, were sharp girls, and she wanted the best for them.

All of these relationships, especially with my dad, had a big influence on my life. I wouldn't realize just how much until years later.

Chapter Two
LIFE IN THE PROJECTS

In the sixth grade, I started sneaking out late to hang out with my new homeboys, the kids from my housing project, to drink and get into trouble. In my neighborhood, there was a park where all the kids would meet up and play. Kids from the Southside and the Northside played together. At that same park, gang members would be there selling drugs, gambling, fighting, and shooting. Yeah that's right, shootings while kids played in the park.

One of the things that appealed to me about drug dealers and big-time gangsters was their low-rider cars with hydraulics and sound systems the entire neighborhood could hear. I was also impressed with their clothes and jewelry. I decided this was something I really wanted to be part of. With a welcoming smile, the older guys in the gang would always say to us as we played, "When are you going to get put on (join) the hood?" or "It's almost that time to get put on."

I looked up to some of the older guys from the hood because they always seemed to show me a lot of love. I looked at them like a father or big-brother figure, even though I was not in the gang. My friends and I would hang out on the front walls. It was a great spot to lay low because we could watch the front gate to see if cops were coming or if anyone was on the attack. We monitored all activities around the hood. It was something to do, and it was exciting.

TROUBLE AT SCHOOL

My attitude continued to worsen. My friends and I, and others in our group that hung together at school, would walk around acting like we were tough. My friend Lee and I were called kings of the school because we made the rules, and other kids looked up to us and respected us.

We would go to three other elementary schools and start fights with the kids there. We would start by playing basketball with them, and then the name calling started, which led to the fighting. This went on for some time. We would march over to these schools, meet up, and have a rumble. But this all came to an end when we arrived at one school and found the teachers were on to us. We had a standoff with the teachers and when they threatened to call the cops, we ran. I was called to the office and suspended. I can hardly believe I behaved this way.

Young kids, especially today, can do some horrible things. Our school was out of control with little violent kids fighting. My teacher, Mr. Patton, could not stand me because I wouldn't listen to him at all. His favorite thing to say to me was, "Tommie, put the pedal to the metal, and get with the program." One day in detention, I became very irritated with him telling me what to do, in what I thought was a mean voice, so I called him a punk. The next thing I knew, he put his hands around my neck and started choking me in front of two other students.

My dad was called because the school couldn't get ahold of my mom. It seemed like he got to the school within a few minutes. The teachers were scared out of their wits when this irate parent stormed through the office looking for Mr. Patton so he could tear him apart. My teacher stood there shaking and the principal had to step in between the two. Mr. Patton got suspended, and that was that. Being choked by my teacher didn't really faze me. I went on starting fights with kids at my school and the surrounding schools. Somehow, through all of that, I graduated from elementary school. My mom was still proud of me and at the same time probably wondered where she went wrong with me. But to me, she was doing her job well. She worked multiple jobs, she loved her kids, and this sometimes broke my heart as I laid my head down on the pillow at night. She never gave up. She cried through the struggles, but my mom was a fighter. Even knowing this, somehow, I couldn't stop my destructive behavior—a prime example of the evil heart of man. Tasha, my older sister, didn't get into much trouble, except for the occasional fight; she was a bit of a tomboy. Tanya, my younger sister, was the square one of the bunch and scared of her own shadow. She was a momma's girl. Still to this day, she is a momma's girl and doing well for herself.

SUMMER TROUBLE

My dad got remarried while in prison, sometime in the mid-80s. He married my stepmother, Beatrice. It took awhile for her and my mother to iron out their differences, but they finally did. Bea was very loving to us (me, Tasha, and Tanya). She called me son, not Tommie, showing her deep love for me. Bea went on to have six daughters: Tommica, Tiffany, Tammy, Tierra, TaToyia, and Tamara. This only added to me being outnumbered already by Tasha and Tanya. Wow, eight sisters! My sisters would try to team up on me, and I would get a butt whooping for throwing them across the room. They were some tough females, straight tomboys.

The 108th Street house we moved into was the first house my dad bought. It was in a gang neighborhood where they wore all green with green bandannas hanging out of their left pockets. The day my dad moved in, he and my cousin Humid were confronted by twenty guys asking them where they were from (what gang). My dad told them which gang he was in and let them know if they tried anything, he and his gang would overrun that neighborhood. So they backed off and after some time, we got to know them a bit.

My sisters would have fights with other girls in the area because they were new to the neighborhood, but later they would come to befriend many of them. Shootings were the norm with other gangs coming over to do drive-bys. The apartment across the street was where one of these gangs lived. It was common for us to have to get on the floor to get out of the way of stray bullets.

I had already started drinking a little at the age of ten. At the age of twelve, the summer before junior high school, I smoked my first joint with my cousin. We had stolen it from one of my aunts.

SOMETHING POSITIVE—SPORTS

At about the same time, I started to make some positive moves. I started playing for a basketball and a football team at Scott Park. My close friend Robert "Robby" Hill and I played well together. Because of our athletic talent, everybody wanted us on their football team. Robby was the quarterback and I was a receiver. On the basketball team, I was a small forward and shooting guard and Robby was the point guard. During our b-ball time, we always made the All-Stars, and one year we made it to a regional-wide tournament and had a chance to play at the sports arena where the Clippers played. We got a chance to meet some of the Clippers and at that time, Danny Manning and Ron Harper were on the team. I was the star of the game and even got an offer for a year's worth of Adidas shoes. If I were to accept the deal, I would have been considered a traitor so I had to turn it down.

While playing sports at Scott Park, I was still involved in criminal activities, although sports started to have a positive influence on me. My next-door neighbor, Victor—who looked just like Magic Johnson—was about seven years older than me. He took a liking to me and gave me all kinds of encouragement about life and my talent for sports. He taught me all about the game of basketball. Victor was more than a friend. He was a big brother to me, and I respected him with all my heart. I attribute some of my character and strengths to Vic. His sister, Zee Zee, was on the girls' team that played at the sports arena. His dad played on a navy basketball team, and he would always talk about his time playing with the Harlem Globetrotters. There was no doubt that this family had sports in their blood.

MY GANG INITIATION

Still, in the midst of all this good, I somehow continued gravitating toward gang life. I was gaining a better understanding of their operations. I learned how to bag up marijuana for sales. One night while I was walking home from my friend Lee's house on the north side of my neighborhood, I took a shortcut through the park area. There stood OG SK, one of the guys I looked up to, with ten other guys who were drinking. He said, "Li'l Tommie, come here." They called me Li'l Tommie because there was another Tommy whose nickname was Capone #3; he was my big sister Tasha's boyfriend.

Laughing, he said, "It's that time." The first blow to my jaw was a quick one, and I went down without a chance to swing back. Many kicks and punches followed. After the initiation beating, I didn't say anything. I just got up and went home with a big lip, sore jaw, and grass in my hair from my head being stomped in the ground. I made it home and as I stumbled my way up the stairs to my room, my mom seemed to appear out of the darkness. She asked, "Are you drunk?" I turned around, and she was shocked by my appearance. I told her I fell off the handlebars of a bike, but she didn't buy it.

Now that I had gotten jumped into this gang, I had to start what we called, "putting in work" or "doing dirt"—various crimes, shooting, fighting other gangs. I tagged walls in the hood with my new nickname, Hit man. They called me Hit man because I was quiet but dangerous. You can also say, young and dumb.

My friend Lee got jumped a little later, and we both went on missions terrorizing the neighborhood, attacking people we didn't know and threatening the security that tried to patrol our hood. We were jumping other kids into the gang and going to other neighborhoods doing mean and crazy things to people. However, in our normal daily activities, we would shoot dice, go over to girls' houses, and sell weed and cocaine. Then we'd be home for dinner. Just about every time I would go over to Lee's house, his mom would say her piece, but she knew that she had no control over him or us. She hated that we were gangbangers, although at times I think she actually liked me and a couple others Lee hung out with.

Lee and I never separated. He would kill anybody for me if it came down to that, and I would have done the same for him. We went on to have shoot-outs with rival gangs. Lee thought he was unstoppable. He would go into our enemies' hoods as if they were his own, and he would pay the price for that. He was shot on several occasions but not killed. In the hood, everybody had a close friend, but Lee was like my brother.

Chapter Three
REIGN OF TERROR AT SCHOOL

Now that summer was over, I was about to start junior high school. I was also about to start a new reign of terror at school and in the community. Carnegie Junior High was a school that had Crips, Pirus, Bloods, and Mexican gangs from the surrounding areas. Junior high was the recruitment grounds for each gang, which included a battle to see who was the strongest gang. My gang was the most hated because we started most of the fights. All the gangs carried weapons with them at all times—knives, hammers, machetes, anything that could be used to hurt someone. With my older homeboys moving on to high school, it was my turn to represent our hood at the junior high. I had started recruiting people but nobody was jumped in yet—just a bunch of wannabes. So I would boss them around telling them who to fight, who to jump, and who to rob. Guys from rival gangs didn't like me much, so we would fight each other. If killing was necessary, then we were ready to go there. With my school having such a bad reputation, the dean tried to help us. Instead of us stabbing or shooting each other, he would let us gang members fight in the gym a few rounds. We didn't tell on him because we respected him for understanding that we had to get things off our chests. It helped a little in stopping riots at school, but it didn't stop the beefs our gangs had outside of school.

It seemed every day something caused us to get out of control. One day a new kid enrolled in our school. He was from a Compton Crip gang that none of us got along with. We attacked him right away, and he didn't tell on us. In fact, the next day he brought a gun to school and showed it to someone. The teachers found out he had it, and he was arrested and taken to jail. This was the norm for schools in South Central LA. If someone felt his life was in danger at school, he would go to his bigger homeboys for a gun if he didn't already have one. So many shootings and stabbings happened at school. A life of destruction and chaos seemed to always be our model, which explains why I got kicked out of several schools in the LA Unified School District: Carnegie Junior High School > Steven White Junior High School > Wilmington Junior High School > Dana Junior High School > Dotson Junior High School.

In my first year at Carnegie, I was kicked out for being involved in too many fights. I was sent to Steven White Junior High where I stayed for a month and was kicked out for fights and starting a riot. I started the riot because I was outnumbered by rival gang members. From there, I was sent to Wilmington Junior High where I would say 99 percent of the gangs were Mexican. I was only there for three days. On the first day, I was approached by a Hispanic gangster from East Side Wilmas in class in front of the teacher. He asked me where I was from—in other words, what gang. The teacher told him to get out of the class and go to the office. He made some racist comments as he left the classroom. On the second day, I received another warning from another Mexican gang member from West Side Wilmas, a different gang that was friendlier to my gang. He told me of the death threats and coming attack from all the gang members in the school. There were only a handful of black students. Two black girls in a gang called Pueblos Bloods stood up in class and said they would fight with me. I'll never forget that—two girls and me against an army. They were two of the most fearless girls I've ever crossed paths with.

The third day for me was the day I was run out of that school. As I was walking up a flight of stairs on my way to class, I heard a bunch of people running up behind me. When I turned around, it looked like twenty or thirty Wilmas gang members coming at me. Somehow, I fought my way past them, ducking and guarding my face from the blows, although they hit me what seemed like a million times. I made it to the office and still several of the gang members stormed into the office after me. A teacher was hit in the process. One of the teachers locked me in one of the rooms in the office. I thought my life was about to end. The security guard waited a few hours trying to get ahold of my mom and when he couldn't, he escorted me to a back gate. I ran for several miles all the way home.

Next, the school district sent me all the way to the city of San Pedro to attend Dana Junior High School where trouble continued to follow me. A Mexican gang that hated and killed blacks, even hung a Crip from a tree, confronted me.

At Dana Junior High School, my life was threatened several times by enemy gangs, and by me standing alone, they pretty much forced me to leave (I got ran out). My mom had me shipped down the street to Dotson Junior High School where I spit on a girl for mouthing off to me on the bus. Her uncle and aunt came to the school and attacked me in the office where I sought safety when I saw them coming for me. The uncle hit me, and I hit him back. Then the aunt grabbed an office phone and hit me with it. A teacher grabbed me, locked me in a room, and the aunt hit the teacher as she tried to get to me.

KICKED OUT OF SCHOOL

At this point, I was kicked out of The LA Unified School District and sent home. My mother was so sad and disappointed. But my cold heart couldn't fully comprehend her sorrow, even though I loved my mom, and she had been there for me all my life not wavering one bit. She took care of me the best she could. For the past twenty years, she has been the best mom in the world.

The 1993 Watts Riot hit the streets in light of the Rodney King beating. Blacks were mad because of the police brutality leading up to the Rodney King beating and for what happened to King. Oh, we hated white folks, and we looked like little ignorant kids. We looked for white people to beat up, and we chased a few down. Like idiots, we looted our own—black-owned—stores instead of focusing on white-owned businesses.

The next day after the riots, the cops went door to door searching houses for stolen goods. America didn't seem like America at this time. I remember feeling like a little revolutionary—us against the world. I thought that the world hated our guts, so I was angry and wanted to hurt someone. I wanted payback.

It is strange the feelings that form in a kid's heart, a kid who is trying to understand the reality of a confusing and violent time in history. Shortly after, a gang peace treaty took place in Watts where people from several different gangs came in an effort to make peace. The National Guard was called in, and they were on the rooftops looking down upon the meetings and ready to fire if need be. With all the police brutality, it caused the Bloods and Crips to unite for a whole three months. It was hard for people who had killed each other daily to get along, considering the fact that kids, mothers, and fathers had been murdered.

Unfortunately, things for me got worse. Over the following summer, my crime spree started. A Mexican gang member taught me how to pop the steering column in a car to steal it, and that's what I did. The first car I stole only took two minutes. But I did not know how to drive, and it was raining. This mission turned out to be a roller coaster. As soon as my friend and I started driving, I slammed on the brakes fast because of a red light I saw at the last minute. Because of the rain, I rammed the car in front of me. The people inside the car yelled at me to pull over, but I backed up and hopped on the freeway. They chased us for a while until we flashed a gun at them to back off. I then drove back to the hood. As the week went on, I stole five more cars. During one of those car thefts, the owner caught me red handed, but he ran back in the house.

I used some of the cars I stole to drive to Magic Mountain, Knott's Berry Farm, or pick up a date, or rob somebody. And, oh yes, I got caught driving one of those stolen cars and was taken to the police station in handcuffs. Right before I got caught, we were driving around different hoods where we knew people—gangs we were cool with—just to show off. On our way out, the cops had the streets blocked off like we had just robbed a bank. They made us get out, put our hands on our heads, and get on our stomachs. The cops called my mom. The judge gave me community service, three years' probation, and a gang prevention program where I had to go to the police station and sit in a counseling session. Grounded by day but sneaking out at night was my motto for the next several months.

Chapter Four

THE LIFE OF CRIME
CONTINUES

We hung out on the block with music blasting, selling drugs, drinking Cisco, and Thunder Bird mixed with Kool Aid, and there was always someone drinking a forty-ounce. Shooting dice and smoking blunts was an everyday, all-day thing. We were high all day. In fact, the only time I left the block was to go to my dad's, to school, or to the movies and the beach with my beautiful mom.

Some school friends invited my sisters and me to a party, which was in the turf of a neighboring gang. There was a cover charge and since I didn't have any money at the time, I had to sneak in. I couldn't believe how many beautiful girls were there. I felt like my heart was going to beat out of my chest. But all my scary butt did was sit near the wall. Besides, gangsters don't dance; we boogie, and they weren't boogying. The movements they did were nasty in my opinion—nasty, but appealing at the same time.

After the party, I separated from my sister and started walking home with a friend from my neighborhood. We were drunk and broke as a joke, so we came up with a plan to start looking for someone to rob. I put on my black hoodie and stalked my prey. When he spotted me, he ran over to someone's house yelling, "Help!

Help!" I ran over to him as if I had a gun under my shirt and told him to give up his money. He did. The Bible tells us that we will reap what we sow (Galatians 6:7). And reap I did. You will see that later.

During the weeks that followed the robbery, there was a lot of turmoil. My homeboys and I would look for trouble. We would go to malls where we knew enemies would be hanging out and start fights. My homeboy Knockout—he could beat up a grown man with no problem—in most cases, would be the one throwing the first punch. I'll never forget the time when we got our Brick Cell phone, which didn't even work, taken from us by this big Samoan Blood gang member. We walked through his park, so he had to show us that we couldn't just walk through like that. He had just gotten out of jail. I guess he thought because we were teenagers we couldn't go and get our whole gang to back us up. But we did. We came back in four cars with our big homeboys, and they evenly matched us. My friend Knockout, at only fifteen years old, badly beat down that twenty-one-year-old buff guy. He didn't have the nickname Knockout for nothing.

The following night my world would come crashing down on me. The guy I had robbed lived in my neighborhood and had been waiting for the right time to call the cops. He somehow knew who I was and sure enough when he spotted me drinking my beer on the block, two police cars surrounded me, and the officers drew their guns. I was on my way to jail. It turns out I would have to face the same judge at the Compton Court Building that I had faced for the stolen car. I was convicted. As I headed to sentencing, the man I had robbed was there on the elevator with me. He said he forgave me and wanted me to come to his house and eat dinner with him and his family so he could talk to me. I couldn't go to his house for dinner because what happened after our elevator meeting changed all that. The judge was steaming mad. The judge's statement was that I was a menace to society, and he sentenced me to six months in a juvenile camp. Then two cops cuffed me. My mom and stepmom, Bea, were there crying, and my dad, who was also in the courtroom, was so disappointed.

JUVENILE JAIL

My first stop was Los Padrinos Juvenile Hall. As the police van pulled up at the jail, I saw two big gates. I called them the gates of hell because I was terrified. My tough-guy attitude went right out the window. No one knew I felt like a scared and sad puppy; I hoped I could somehow be made invisible. After being unloaded from the transit van, they called out the names and units we would be going to and mine was L&M. Immediately, terror struck my heart—no mom, no warm bed. I thought I was about to be on a fighting rampage because every street gang and every race I hated was in the same building. I was a target for them as well. It was on! Or as we say in LA, "It's on and crackin'."

I made it to Unit L&M. This unit would be my home for the next few months before I would head to Camp Rocky, a lockdown camp for the most hard-headed. As I walked into the unit, the first face I saw was a very big Mexican gangster with a face I'll never forget. Half of his face was sagging because there was no bone on that side. He also had a large tattoo that covered his whole face with "18th Street," which was the largest Hispanic gang in the country at that time. He asked me where I was from. In gang language, I got "hit up." That's what we did on the street or in jail; we hit people up. If we crossed paths with others who seemed to gangbang, we hit them up to make sure we didn't have to beat them, shoot them, or rob them. This guy didn't have a problem with me and went on his way. I had no further problem with him.

My cell was very small. It had a small window, brick walls, and a skinny mat for a bed that I could roll up. It was colder than a polar bear's toenail in that cell. My cellmate was Scooby from Watts Varrio Grape St. He was one of the coolest Mexicans I ever met, and he didn't want to fight me. His mindset was "I just wanna do my time and that's it." He made us some dice out of tissue, and we gambled for pushups during lockdown hours. Outside of the cell we couldn't really hang out because of our ethnic backgrounds. It was just prison politics.

The next day I was let out for a routine doctor checkup and enrollment in school, which was standard for newbies. While waiting for the doctor, an inmate who had already been to jail in the past told me that I should take a pencil from school and sharpen it for protection. My heart dropped to my feet. I was truly awakened to the fact that this wasn't a dream. I went into defense mode. I knew I couldn't show any sign of weakness . . . at all.

In my unit, we had a day room with a bunch of chairs, a TV, and board games. The day room was where we took out all the anger we had bottled up. Fights were a daily activity. The first fight I saw was with a kid named AWOL from Atlantic Drive Compton Crip and the guy with the 18th Street on his face. Racial slurs passed back and forth, and next thing we knew the guard was spraying us all with pepper spray. We had to strip down and get in the shower—all together—which was something we did daily anyway. It's just part of being locked up. We were like cattle—eating together, using the restroom together, showering together, and watching TV together. That is, when we were told we could do so.

My time of testing finally came. One of the Hispanic kids challenged me to a fight because he wanted to sit in the seat I sat in daily to watch TV. Seats were assigned by us inmates. I had a spot to call my own; that was my seat. I came out of my cell and found this kid named Owl in my seat, and I simply asked him to move. He got in my face and said to meet him in his cell. Meeting in the cell was something we did to get out of the sight of the guards so we could get a good fight in before being stopped. The rumble was on! I was pretty nervous because it was my first jail term. But one thing I couldn't do was back down, or I would be considered "wolf food" to the rest of the inmates. I gave him the beat down he wanted, and that was that. Many other things took place at Los Padrinos Juvenile Hall, including a late-night visit from my dad. One of the homeboys he grew up with was a guard there. I was shocked and happy to see my pops and the big burrito and soda he brought!

After a few months at LP, I was shipped to Sylmar Juvenile Hall Detention Center. It was just a place to process before going to Camp Rocky, and it was a lot cleaner than the old LP jail. I stayed there for two days in the hole. It was a twenty-three-hour lockdown and two torturous days at Sylmar. I was locked in the same cell with a kid who cried for forty-eight hours straight and hit the walls begging to be released. That kid yelled, "I wanna go home, I wanna go home! I can't take this!" He said that over and over again until I grabbed him, shook him, and told him, "It's not going to happen. You're not going home!" Come to find out, he was only going to be in for a week. When he told me that, I stood in disbelief. This kid was going home in a few days! I guess those walls can get to anybody, even me.

After my two days of torture by this fellow inmate, who was in complete terror and dread of his jail cell, I was shipped for one day to Central Juvenile Hall in Los Angeles. Once there, I sat in a big basketball gym with a couple hundred kids waiting to be shipped to camps. Within just a few hours, several fights broke out. There were enemies everywhere. When the fighting and arguing died down, I went to the restroom where someone was waiting for me. As I entered, I was hit right on the jaw, which made me hit the bathroom wall, and red was all I saw. I turned around to fight back, only to meet a can of pepper spray. I rinsed it off in the shower. Fortunately, we didn't get sent to the hole or locked down because we were going to camp.

Finally, my bus arrived, and I was able to get away from that gladiator arena. Camp Rocky, here I come! Being in that gym was terrible, but a part of me got a thrill out of it. Besides, I knew I wasn't going home for a while so a little action now and then was okay.

Chapter Five

OFF TO CAMP ROCKY

I arrived at a heavily wooded area on top of a mountain in San Dimas. From the outside, it was very beautiful. It reminded me of the area around Big Bear Lake. We finally pulled up to the twenty- or thirty-foot-tall gates with barbed wire on top to prevent escape. The gates opened, and I saw a huge running track in the center, a basketball court, and a table area to the left of the field. All the buildings were in one big circle. Inside the big gate was the main office, the mess hall, our dorm, and the school. The lockdown unit was called "the shoe" or "the box" and was for those who fought or had other mess-ups. Then there was the weight pile for workouts. On the inside, this place looked like the prisons I saw on TV. Once again, my heart dropped to my feet.

I changed into my camp-issued jeans, a white shirt, and a Ben Davis jacket. The staff yelled threats and warnings at us. They assigned us counselors. My counselor was Mr. Abernathy, who reminded me of Uncle Fester from *The Addams Family*. He was a cool guy who seemed to have a genuine concern for me. All eyes were on us new guys. As we walked in to our dorms, we got ugly looks and some threats. As soon as we were assigned to a bunk, they surrounded us asking what gang we were from. Larry Langford, one of my friends I grew up with who was a Crip from Long Beach, was there. On the street, we were pretty close, so I was comforted just a little. The kids there looked like they were on steroids. Two of these guys looked like Incredible Hulks. I found out they stayed in the workout area every day.

The next day following my arrival was my day to face everybody in the facility. They were going to sniff me out, like a dog sniffs another animal, to see what I was about. They also wanted to see what gang I was from—and if I was a wuss—or if I was what we called "active" or "with the business," which simply means not scared.

After all the questions, I had a good report, but not with everybody. Some didn't like me because I wasn't scared of them, and so I had a few fights lined up for later. I had some close friends right away. C-Loc from Caver Park Compton Crip, Green Eyes from Village Town Piru, my friend Larry, and Lump from Spook Town. In there, Bloods and Crips didn't really matter unless you had an arch enemy in the midst and then a fight must take place on sight, or worse, a stabbing.

A few weeks passed, and I got a job working in the laundry room, which was located outside the camp. I had a chance to see some wildlife and also pick up packs of cigarettes that parents would drop on "accident" while coming to visit their kids. It was a great source of wealth for a young street hustler like myself. I had all brand-new jail clothes because of where I worked and unlimited tissue. Man, the things we take for granted, like tissue. I found value in things that I would not have on the outside.

I also attended an unorthodox school at Camp Rocky. My teacher, Mr. Delorca, was the coolest, craziest teacher in the world. He was the coolest because he looked like Steven Segal with a ponytail and a Harley Davidson he rode and parked in the camp. And the craziest because instead of responding to our ignorance, he would simply call us to the middle of the class and tell us to take him out if we could. Many of us tried but failed. This man was crazier than we were. My guess was that he was in a biker gang.

One of the fights I had lined up came to pass. We had a strange way of fighting in there. We had to fight in the restroom, and several inmates had to be in there at the same time. We scheduled the times we had our friends go in ahead of us, and they would turn on the sinks and flush the toilets to cover up the noise of the fight. We would get on our knees and punch each other until someone quit. A kid from West LA School Yard Crip was my first fight. I would say there was no clear winner because we were interrupted, but that kid could fight. I'll give him that. Fight number two was with a kid named Blind Blood from Bounty Hunter Watts Blood. We called him that because of the two-inch-thick glasses he wore. This guy was no push over and was fearless. I was accused of cutting in the nurse's line, he started mouthing off to me, so we started fighting in front of the nurse. We both got sent to the shoe unit for a week. We were only able to wear boxer shorts and it was freezing! All we could do was talk to each other by yelling through the walls for a week.

Following the week of lockdown, we were assigned to rock duty where we broke boulders with pick axes. That was a Hollywood moment for sure. I was called to the main office and a lady asked if I was the son of Tommie Scott from Grape Street Watts and I said yes. She proceeded to show me a newspaper clipping of my dad escaping from Camp Rocky when he was a boy. My dad and his friend carried their metal beds to the wall, stacked them on top of each other, and got away. I was shocked but at the same time, I thought it was cool.

GOING HOME TO MORE VIOLENCE

It was finally time for my release, and I was happy to be going home. I was tired of all the fights and most of all, I missed home. Mr. Abernathy gave the okay to release me, and I was free at last. I wondered what would be next as my mom and I drove down the highway and headed home. I didn't want to ever go back to that place! I was kicked out of LA Unified School District. I had a record. My friends were locked up or dead. I didn't get along with some of my friends because they weren't anywhere to be found when I was in jail. Challenges were on the horizon.

When I was away in jail, my friend Lee was shot on three different occasions. The third time he died from the gunshot wound. When he died, he had twenty or more bullets in his body from previously being shot. Understandably, his mom hated my guts. In fact, she hated everyone in the neighborhood. This tragic death of my close friend really affected me. I became even more numb to death. I wasn't scared to die. I didn't cry at funerals, and my emotions seemed to have left my body. It was hard to cry even at funerals for family members. It had affected my conscience. I was like a dead man walking—no feelings at all.

The murder rate in LA was increasing. I witnessed death firsthand. I saw a guy in the alley with his neck slit. Along with other eyewitnesses, there was a killing in broad daylight with all the kids outside playing. A little girl was killed in a drive-by shooting while riding her bike. I was in many shoot-outs defending my life from rival gangs. I'll spare you the details because my goal is not to scare you but to wake you up to the reality of precious life dropping like flies right here in America from crime, drugs, and gangs. I am writing this to show the saving power of Jesus Christ and that wherever your life is right now, there is hope.

My decline in caring for other people's feelings increased. Even after juvenile hall and Camp Rocky, it was like I could not escape who I had become. Darkness and deviousness came through my pores. My mom wanted to move us from the projects because of the danger I was in. I had become a wanted man. People wanted me dead. So we moved to the Lakewood area of Long Beach, about thirty minutes away from our old neighborhood. But it was still LA County.

LA County was a gang cesspool. "Countywide, CAL/GANG estimates there are 1,108 gangs with 85,298 members,"[2] and that's not including all the various cliques and gang off-shoots. I already knew trouble would follow very soon, even if my mom didn't know

[2] Richard Winton, "L.A. Home Turf for Hundreds of Neighborhood Criminal Groups," *Los Angeles Times*, (May 13, 2005): http://articles.latimes.com/2005/may/13/local/me-explainer13

it. I thought it was kind of a neutral area, meaning it was more about just making money. I was wrong. The area was run by Khaos Mob, a hybrid gang with Crips and Bloods from all over LA County. A guy named Tic Loc was from Holmes Street Watts, and he was the head of Khaos Mob in that area. But the Khaos Mob had many cliques around LA. I joined forces with them because the big threat was a Hispanic gang in the next city over called Hawaiian Gardens 13. They were a very racist group like many other Hispanic gangs in LA. They would kill little old black ladies and even young black kids who were still in school. They hated us so much. They say gang life is about drugs, and that's part of it, but I say it's just plain hate. Now I realize that it was not only hate, but demonic.

In Southern California, it's always been a black against Mexican thing, but both sides always had their internal problems. At first, there were some blacks in Mexican gangs and Mexicans in black gangs. But the Mexican Mafia banned blacks from their street gangs. Besides, it was hard for them to live in California prisons where inmates are segregated if not by the prison by each other.

Now that I was home, all day and all night we would hang out, drink, smoke weed, and listen to X-Raided, Brotha Lynch Hung, and 2-Pac, the three rappers who rapped about our kind of life. We understood them and did the same things they rapped about. Not to say that they really *did* them, but we could relate. We would look for anybody we didn't know to come to 216th St. We would chase them down, rob, and beat them if we didn't know them because this was our street.

Chapter Six

BRING NEW LIFE INTO THE WORLD

In the neighborhood, I became friends with three brothers—Hoova Tyson, T-Capone, and T-Man—and two were from 52nd St. Hoova Criminal Gang in South Central. They would later become my brothers-in-law and partners in crime.

Their sister Antoinette would bear my first two children. Antoinette had a loving heart. We hit it off great. She already had kids but that was okay. I came to love them deeply. Our first child was Tommiya, my daughter, who is now twelve years old. Next was Li'l Tommie, our son, who is now ten. But after three-and-a-half years, Antoinette and I broke up.

At this point, my dad, Bea, and my six half sisters moved from South Central LA to Moreno Valley, which is about forty-five minutes from LA. A lot of people from LA started moving to the outskirts to get away from the gangs, violence, over population, and horrible traffic. But us LA folks brought our troubles, gangs, and violence with us wherever we went.

My sisters, having grown up in South Central, had no tolerance for any disrespect from other kids. My sisters were like a gang within themselves. We had become very close, so close that the word "half" was never used between my six sisters, Bea, and me. Bea was just a second mother to me.

The eight girls, with all their friends, were a force to be reckoned with at school or wherever we went. They had multiple rumbles. At a major theme park like Knott's Berry Farm or Magic Mountain we would have a big fight by the end of the night, and the whole theme park would come to a halt to stop us—me and my gangsta family. We got a kick out of it. That's just how it was. My dad would take our whole family and friends to these places, but we couldn't function like normal people. We were far from a normal family, except for my saintly mom who didn't come with us.

I had been living with one of my aunts at this time, which was fun. However, I had two beautiful children who needed their dad, and I needed money to take care of my babies. Without a job, it was impossible to do that. So I decided to join my dad's line of work.

WORKING WITH DAD

During the times my dad was home, he had a team of street professionals he had worked with for many years. Long story short, I joined my dad's team after months and months of begging him to let me join. I told him that he should understand where I was coming from. After all, I had a record, two kids, and I knew he wasn't just going to let them starve. I knew my dad's heart. He couldn't turn down friends who needed him, so I knew he couldn't say no to me.

So it began. I joined him and made thousands of dollars. I bought a brand-new car—a Camaro with a Corvette engine in it. I was going to buy a house but didn't. Right away, I started wasting money, treating friends to drugs and drinks, and paying their way into clubs to party. Just doing stupid things with the money and my life. One week after buying the car, I crashed into a tree driving home drunk from a club. The engine was all the way in the front seat of the car with me. I was knocked out by the impact. I got out okay but as a result, today I continue to struggle with back problems.

THE LOVE OF MY LIFE

With my car and money gone, my dad kept me out of the loop of things because he couldn't trust me. It gave me more time to capture the heart of my sister Tommica's beautiful friend Rache't (pronounced Are-Shay). I thought Rache't was a dark chocolate smoothie, just sweet. She grew up in Compton but moved to Moreno Valley like the rest of us. Her mom and dad came from the ghettos of Compton. The time came for them to move to a safer area because they had two beautiful girls to raise. They raised two ladies: Rache't, my future wife, and Latasha, her older sister. There was just something about Rache't that made me crazy. One day, I finally told my sister to tell her that I wanted to call her.

Rache't would come over to my dad's house in these beautiful dresses and skirts that would drive me absolutely mad. I couldn't get her off my mind. I would hang around the house and hope that she would come over with my sister after they let out of school.

Rache't had this diva attitude, but at the same time she was meek and very much a lady. She was also a smart and witty girl who always knew what she wanted. She had a powerful personality with a beautiful smile. People always complimented her. I was like a little kid all over again when I was around her. I felt like a new man with new confidence when I was with her. I felt respected and loved with no strings attached. It felt like I was in a dream. Rache't was, and is still, my backbone. I would be dead if she wouldn't have put up with my stuff. As we developed our friendship, we both knew we were to be together forever. She was a gift from God.

Because my father kept me out of the loop, I had arguments with him, and eventually I packed my bags and moved back to Long Beach to live with my mom and sister Tanya. My other sister Tasha left for the army after I arrived.

I had been visiting my friends each month because it wasn't too far to travel to see them in LA or around LA. Since I had been gone, Tic Loc had gotten a job working for the Long Beach Town Center Wal-Mart. He somehow worked me in and got me hired. It was my first real job, and I caught on pretty fast because I was a hustler. Dealing with people was easy and having a job didn't slow me down one bit.

I ALMOST DIED

I continued with my daily doings—drinking, hanging out, just causing trouble. You've heard the saying: what goes around comes around. Well, for all the people and families I hurt, I was about to reap what I had sown. One night after getting off work a friend of mine, Greedy Loc, who Tic Loc and I was grooming to be a street solider, picked me up and we stopped at a liquor store to get some beers and cigars to roll our weed up in. At this time, the black and Mexican gangs were at war with one another.

Mexicans in our area shot and killed any blacks they saw. Gang members were the target, but sometimes the innocent got hurt. A Mexican club, next to the liquor store, was packed and the parking lot full of people. Some gang members spotted us. At first, we didn't know until we saw them pacing back and forth outside the store. So I told Greedy to buy us some gloves because we were about to fight. Making our way out of the store, we were confronted in the doorway, blocking us from leaving the store. I could tell right away that one of them was drunk and high on something. The sober one had a big gun by his side pointed to the ground. He seemed quiet and level headed, while the racial slurs and ranting about his gang came out of the high one's mouth. He was so close to me that I thought about snatching the gun out of the calm one's hand. Suddenly, the wild one pulled out a long army knife and stabbed me in the belly, cutting upward and slicing right next to my heart. I ran back into the store, bleeding all over the place, yelling for the store owner to call for help. She gave Greedy[3] a chair and made us sit back outside. It

---

[3] Greedy Loc ended up serving a ten-year sentence in a California state prison. Some of my influence into his way of life sent him, and countless others, there with him.

hurt so bad. It felt like ten people were sitting on my chest. I would have rather been shot than stabbed in the stomach.

The paramedics got there quick. As I lay in the back of the ambulance, I didn't know how badly I had been hurt. I just knew I couldn't breathe, and I didn't know if I would make it. I just thought of my family and my kids.

The word that I had been stabbed made its way to most of my friends and family. They crowded into the hospital. The only thing I remember in the hospital was the doctor giving me meds and telling me to count to ten backward; almost immediately I was out. After the operation, I woke up to my family yelling my name. I said, "What are y'all looking at?" and went back to sleep.

My friends were mad and wanted to go and do something to these people, but I guess I prevented them. I didn't file any charges. That's just not the way we did things on the streets. Snitching could get you and your family killed, and hundreds have died for snitching. That's a fact.

After being discharged from the hospital, I went back to work. The wife of the guy who stabbed me found out where I worked, came to the store with her kid, and apologized. She asked me not to take her husband to court; otherwise, the kids wouldn't be able to see their dad if he was convicted. I told her that's not what we do in the hood. I have no idea how she found out where I worked. I started to feel like I had been set up, but I'll never know that for sure.

Chapter Seven

GET OFF THE CELL PHONE!

My dad wouldn't let me continue hustling with him, but I had something else in mind. I could just teach someone the methods I had learned from my pops. That's just what I did. I got my boy "Boo" who was from our clique. Boo was a cool homey. I thought we could make some quick money together. As I was robbing a store, Boo was on his cell phone paying no attention to his surroundings. I came across a fist full of money in a back office drawer, and so I kept looking for more money not knowing that the silent alarm was going off. I happened to see the front security light go off, a.k.a. "the snitch light." I ran to the back of the store only to see a police truck coming up the alley and Boo talking on the cell phone while I was committing the crime. I told him the cops were coming. I turned around only to see the barrel of a gun pointed at me and a female officer yelling, "Get down on the ground!" I was on my way to jail with my roll of hundreds gone. I was so sick to my stomach and could have strangled Boo.

COUNTY JAIL

I was an adult and by now, I had been to many county jails—all of the LA County jails and a Riverside County jail. Now it was time to try out Orange County Jail. As I entered the booking area, I realized there were not many blacks in this jail. Being from Southern California, there are a lot of jail and prison politics dealing with race issues, so being outnumbered meant trouble.

With my record, I figured that the courts would be swift with me and send me to prison, a place where I hadn't been yet. I heard a lot of stories about prison and oh, the terror that was in my heart! Orange County Jail was a strange land. Not only was I outnumbered racially, but I was from another county so I wouldn't know anyone there.

It was a dorm setting. In all my jail life, I had never been around such a strange group of men. We had the "wood pile" (the white boys); the "Southsiders" (the Mexicans) all from different hoods of Southern California Hispanic gangs; "the Brothers" (the blacks), which included Bloods, Crips, and neutrals; and the "others" (Asians, Native Americans, and other ethnic groups). This dorm had a long hallway with beds on each side of the walls—a brick wall on one side and bars on the other. Outside the bars was a walkway with a large, one-sided window of glass where the guards monitored us day and night. Our beds were separated by race so that fights were limited as much as possible. The first few weeks were all about absorbing the fact that I wasn't going home for a while.

We were on lockdown because of several attacks on officers. Inmates were throwing sheets over the heads of officers and then attacking them. With this going on, it was a sure bet that the officers had a chip on their shoulder.

While going back and forth to court, my stress increased and all I did was eat, drink coffee, and sleep. I wasn't really too talkative at first until things started to happen. Riots between the whites and Mexicans were rare. They usually did business together and had each other's backs on most issues. As tensions boiled over, the blacks began experiencing racism from the guards and the white and the

Hispanic inmates. We were the bottom of the barrel so to speak. We would get into arguments over the nasty things they allowed to happen out in the open, things that would be offensive to any man.

One morning prior to going to breakfast, the cell doors opened and on the lower tier we could hear someone yelling and cursing at a guard. We looked down and saw a man lying on his bed with a blood-soaked white sheet over him. The guards strolled in like nothing was wrong, even after they saw the man there stiff and not moving. The inmates started spitting on the guards, yelling out threats. The guards used stun guns, pepper spray, and rubber bullets. Lockdown was in effect.

Lockdown wasn't too bad in a dorm setting. The whole unit stayed up all night clowning, drinking coffee, and rapping. In fact, as I loosened up, I joined the 2:00 a.m. rap circles, and I can't even rap. But you couldn't tell me that. I was getting things off my chest and trading war stories at the same time.

We had a fight area where we would have one-on-one fights. All I would hear were bodies hitting the walls, smacks from fists, and I saw black eyes and swollen jaws and lips. One night, the guards let in an inmate who had mental issues. He was clearly in the wrong building. He would get in the shower at three or four in the morning, and the shower was right next to the black bunks. We made our complaints to the white shot caller (the leader), and he was told to stop for a couple of days. He didn't stop, so they thought they were just going to beat him down. This guy with the mental issues beat the living day lights out of these two big, tattooed, biker-gang-looking dudes. I thought, *Whaaaat just happened!* They were shocked and didn't know what to do next, so they told the guards to roll him up (get him out of our unit).

SENTENCED TO PRISON

Sentencing day had arrived, and I was sentenced to a year and six months in a California state prison. While waiting for my transfer to prison, I asked the older inmate, who had already been to prison, a million questions about what to expect. When my transfer came through, I packed up my things and was on my way up state for my first prison term. I would be lying if I said I was not nervous.

While on the way to Wasco State Prison, they played oldies over the radio, and it felt like I was doomed, never to return. With my temper, I knew I was either going to be hurt or I was going to hurt someone. I didn't like being told what to do by another inmate shot caller. I think prison is kind of like the military where you have no choice but to play by the rules. I just knew it was a matter of time before I blew up and went off on somebody. In prison, you are either going to mind somebody or be wolf food.

The Wasco State Prison reception area had a circle of cells with people inside being processed like cattle. We were just another number in the system waiting our turn to get a number and an ID badge. This took all day. I lay on the concrete floor with others who were there serving anywhere from two to a hundred years. I even met a guy serving two hundred years. Like he could really live that long. At first, they sent me to the twenty-three-hour a day lockdown yard where the lifers were housed—kids from eighteen all the way to eighty years old, for various crimes like murders, armed robberies, and home invasions. I sure wasn't about to tell them how much time I had. My cellmate was an eighteen-year-old kid from 51 Trouble Gang in South Central. This kid could sing and rap while making beats on his chest, legs, or wherever he could make a beat. At the same time, he talked about how he would be a smarter gangsta when he got out in eighteen years and how he was going to teach his younger homeboys how to do it right. He was more disturbed than I was. He was in for a very violent crime.

It was an eerie cellblock. Many of them were never going home again. They would never have a chance to sleep, eat, or use the restroom when they wanted. This was the reality for those who had chosen the path I was on. It's always all fun and games until you get caught. The fast life. So fast your life can be over at eighteen, either living in a cell by yourself or having to live with another man for the rest of your life.

After a week, they transferred me over to the C Yard where lower convictions went. The yard looked like a warehouse. There were about two hundred people in this unit in orange jumpsuits and karate shoes or shower shoes. There were two big TVs with benches in front of them and of all things on TV, they were watching *Cops*. While sitting on my assigned bed, inmates would quietly walk by and ask me where I was from. They did things more respectfully in prison than in county jail. Even the guards showed a certain level of respect. This was a don't-shoot-yourself-in-the-foot deal. The black representative came over to show me what sinks were black and what showers and toilets were ours. We even had our own workout area and chow tables in the prison yard. The guard podium stood in the center so they could view the whole building. So far, everything was running smoothly. During my first week on C Yard, there were no stabbings or anything strange. Naturally, that would change.

With this only being the reception yard, I figured that most would be on relax mode because we were all going to be shipped to different prisons anyway. But no, like any jail, people fought over the stupidest things. A black guy from Fresno took it upon himself to move a white guy's prison ID from his seat. We would put our IDs down to save a seat in front of the TV, and everyone knew that to touch somebody's ID, especially from another race, was a big no-no. It was against the rules, and it could start a riot.

When this man realized his ID had been moved by a black guy, he went over to his representative (leader) and reported what had happened. This was on New Year's Eve, and we all had cups of home-brewed alcohol called pruno.[4] Things got quiet, and you could cut the tension in the air with a knife. I could sense a war about to break out. About fifty of us blacks grouped up for battle. The leader came over and told us that we had to discipline our people. What that meant was we had to beat down our guy in order to prevent a riot. There was complete silence.

---

[4] Different fermented fruits with a lot of added sugar.

An older prisoner from the 83 Hoover Gang and I were the first ones on the front line for battle. We handled the whole situation together, and this earned me a great deal of respect from others. I didn't talk all the time, and I was quick to get in the mix of things. We asked the guy from Fresno, who had started the whole thing, if he wanted us to jump him or kick off a riot. We gave him a choice, even though he was wrong and could have been responsible for a lot of people going down with more time. He was a champ and took one for the team. Before the riot team got into place, we let them know we were about to discipline one of our people and they said, "Just hurry up." I was shocked. This was all new to me. We lumped him up pretty good, and so the beef was squashed.

Soon I was back on the yard jogging, playing b-ball, and socializing, waiting to be transferred to the main prison where I was to be housed. We still had to sleep with our shoes on because after an event like that any little mess up in word or deed could pull the trigger, and it would be riot time.

I was finally called to roll my things up. The bus was there to transfer me to the prison where I would spend the rest of my time. What anguish and dread I felt not knowing what to expect. Was I going to have to be tested or kill somebody? What was I about to get into?

I was born in Los Angeles in 1980. Here I am at age three with my dad and little sister, Tanya. This was right before my mom and pops split up for good, and Mom would set out on her journey of raising us on her own.

I grew up in the projects. This was where my life took a dark turn into gangs, drugs, and violence.

As early as the elementary school years, I lashed out against authority, which kept me in detention and at home on suspension.

Los Padrinos Juvenile Hall, Downey, CA. I stayed here for a few months before heading off to Camp Rocky.

Mom visited me regularly in what would be my home for the next two years—the California Department of Corrections.

At the Clark County Detention Center in Las Vegas, Nevada, I had an encounter with the risen Christ—Jesus, my Lord.

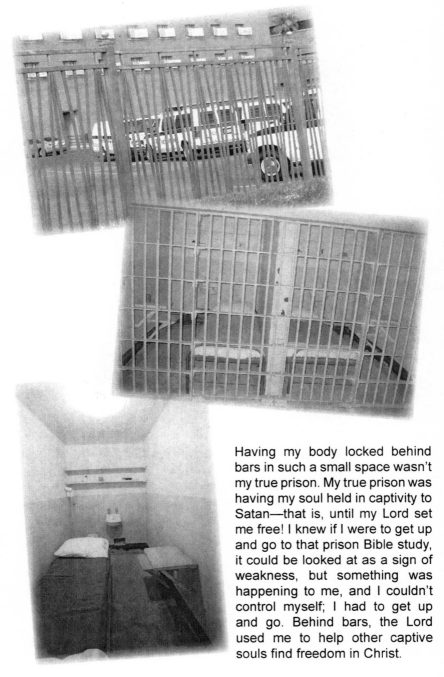

Having my body locked behind bars in such a small space wasn't my true prison. My true prison was having my soul held in captivity to Satan—that is, until my Lord set me free! I knew if I were to get up and go to that prison Bible study, it could be looked at as a sign of weakness, but something was happening to me, and I couldn't control myself; I had to get up and go. Behind bars, the Lord used me to help other captive souls find freedom in Christ.

Tim Berends

Kleg Seth

The first time I went to the prison Bible study, I met two men—Tim Berends, a Christian radio host known for distributing gospel tracts on the streets of Las Vegas, and Kleg Seth, pastor of Trinity Life Church. Only God could have known then what an impact these two men would have on my life and on my walk with the Lord.

Not long after my release from prison, my girlfriend, Rache't, recommitted her life to Jesus Christ. We were married in 2010, and then we, as husband and wife, were baptized together to demonstrate our commitment to keeping Jesus first in our private lives and in our marriage.

As a new believer, I was fired up for the Lord. I took to the Las Vegas streets and the famous "Fremont Street experience," where I shared the gospel. The Lord led me into ministry with Pastor Kleg Seth, and we worked together at our Tuesday night outreach to inner city, at-risk youth where young men were, and still are, being set free for all of eternity.

It's amazing how God uses us in ways we would never have thought possible. Today I am working on becoming a licensed chaplain, am a member of the Nevada Gang Task Force, and am greatly involved in street evangelism. I go anywhere the Lord wants me to go. It's all for His glory.

Chapter Eight
PRISON BLUES

They made us strip down to our boxers and put on this blue paper disposable jumpsuit. We were off to Coalinga, California. Upon arrival, I could feel my blood pressure go up, and I was ready for whatever came my way. About fifteen of us were put in a small cell and given a bag with an apple and the best sandwich I had in months. People said in county that prison food was good, and they gave you a lot of it. At this prison, they farmed and produced their own milk and artichokes. They gave us some blue jeans, a light blue button-up shirt, and a jacket. These were our "prison blues." This was right before California took the jeans away and started providing orange scrubs with "CDC" printed in bold, black letters on the pants leg and back of the shirt.

As I entered my building, I saw Hispanics playing dominoes with blacks. I thought, *What is this?* I had never seen anything like it. I found out these were Hispanics from Central California called Bull Dog (cool with blacks). In Southern Cali, you have Sureños (Southsiders) with all southern Hispanic gangs united under the Mexican Mafia who hates blacks. And then you have Northern California Norteños (Northsiders) under their mafia, Nuestra Familia (cool with blacks).

This was interesting to see. As I headed over to my bed, blacks from Southern Cali came over to greet me and check me out. In this prison, the only friends I had were the blacks from Southern California. They hooked me up with food and coffee as a welcoming gift and showed me the ropes—areas in the prison that were our areas.

Those of us from Southern California and the blacks from Northern California didn't get along that well as a whole, but I became good friends with a few of them even though they were a weird bunch. At least I thought so. They were loud all the time, but their sense of humor made the time fly by. The things to come would not be so good for me, but I made it through.

Rache't sent me a package with some new shoes, a sweat suit, some white shirts, socks, and a Walkman radio to play my oldies. This made me feel like I had a little freedom.

As I learned to adjust to my environment, the energy there was good. This gave me a lot of time to think about my life. I had kids, and now I was in prison. I remember thinking of myself as just trying to provide for my children. But it was much deeper than that. What was embedded in me were things other than just trying to provide for my kids and be a good dad. There was the bitterness of being hated by other races. Even in the criminal world, we (blacks) were the outcasts, and we hated ourselves as well. There were race issues in my own family. My grandmother's family disowned my grandmother (white) when she married my grandfather (black), who played with the 50s group The Platters. My dad also embedded some racism and hatred in us toward whites and Mexicans. He also told us not to trust our own people because they would cross us if we let them. With all this bottled up in me, I felt as if I couldn't do anything else but hate. I felt stuck and thought even if I tried, the white man wouldn't let me make it in the end. Even if that wasn't the case, my confidence was gone. I didn't feel equal to other people in the world. Even though that's not reality, that's what I and others in many of the communities like mine believed and still do believe.

My heart was broken because my kids were at home without their dad. I couldn't take care of them. They needed me, and I let them down. I hated myself and I felt worthless. I wished I could have snapped my fingers and been a different man for my kids. I didn't even feel like living any more.

RELIGION NOT FOR ME

Right when I start feeling this way, a very tall, older man about six-foot-eight-inches tall with dreadlocks talked to me and encouraged me. I guess he saw that I was young and new to the prison system. He directed me to a church service he was a part of. I attended a few times, but there was nothing there but an escape from reality. I tried Jesus. I tried religion. I found out later that it's not what we do for Christ, but what He has done for us all.

Mr. Dreadlocks was never a forceful guy; he was meek and kind. He was a gentle giant always picking my brain. There was also a Hispanic (ex-Southsider) and another Hispanic (ex-Bull Dog) who were Christians. They were fearless, bold Christians in prison. That kind of caught my attention.

One day I was talking to Chris, one of the Hispanic Christians. We were on the second floor of the unit in front of the staircase looking down on the floor below where the inmates were watching the Laker game. All Chris kept talking about was spiritual warfare, and then a strange thing happened. This is the absolute truth. We were standing on the balcony right next to the stairs. As he spoke, suddenly it was like everything slowed down, and we were in slow motion. We looked down, and this dark green smoke or mist was all around. Shocked, we looked at each other. There was no real explanation for this. Our friendship grew because of this event, which we called "the dark strong hold." But even after that, I still wasn't converted and continued in my ways, although I was always haunted by that experience. Chris wondered why I didn't follow Christ. It was just too much for me to give up everything and everybody I knew. At least that's how I saw it.

THEY WERE MY FRIENDS

I only had about six months left on my sentence. The prison system did something unbelievable when they left four northern Hispanics on the same yard with southern Hispanics. This was something they never did because of their arch rivalry. They hated and killed each other on the streets and in prison. The northern Hispanics were warned by the southern Hispanics for two weeks to roll up their things, go to the gate, and leave. But they chose to stay. The northern and southern blacks were on program with each other. In other words, we ate together, played sports, cards, traded with each other, and did business.

At the end of the two weeks, the northern Hispanics wouldn't leave so the southern Hispanics moved on them and stabbed them to death. I don't know if all died or not. I was both sad and mad because before they were attacked, we were with them each day. The northern blacks wanted to back them up, but some southern blacks didn't want to help. I did because in many other prisons they were our allies.

I got mad and started a fight with a couple of blacks from Southern Cal. I got sent to the hole for thirty days for fighting. This also started internal fighting with northern blacks against southern blacks.

A VISIT WITH RACHE'T AND TYLON

After being released from the hole, I had a visit from my mom, my girl, Rache't, and our one-year-old-son, Tylon. As I heard my name being called for visits, my heart started beating fast, and I couldn't even think straight from all the excitement. I rarely got visits because I was so far away, but seeing them gave me strength to finish the time I had left. The comfort of my mom, the beautiful smile and smell of perfume on Rache't, and the big eyes and presence of Tylon was the best time of my life at that point. All the things I took for granted, all the wasted time, and the lives I damaged was because of my foolish and evil deeds. The visit was wonderful.

As we were stripped bare for the guards to search us for drugs or anything being smuggled in from the visit, all I could think of was going home with them, going back to my house and my bed. I felt loved. This helped to keep me in check for the rest of my time.

I called the basketball games on the yard a sort of UFC/NBA because it was rough play. It's weird; the guys are in tip-top shape, yet they can't play ball. So we would get slammed into the wall or get tackled to the ground by someone trying to stop us from scoring.

I enrolled in some classes because it got me good time, which meant I could get time knocked off my sentence. I took a Microsoft Windows course and a release program, and both classes were helpful. They were also fun because it kept my mind on something else for the time being. It felt like a mini vacation.

Finally, my counselor sent for me to come to his office so that we could talk about my upcoming release date in a few months. We talked about my goals for the future. He told me to sign up for a prison release class that would equip me for the outside.

OH HAPPY DAY!—MY RELEASE

My release was finally here, and Rache't and her best friend, Kandyce, were there to pick me up. I was so excited I could barely put my clothes on right. I got my two-hundred-dollar exit money and headed for the front gate. Clowning, as I walked through the gate, I fell to my knees and said, "I'm free!" The best part? Unrestricted hugs and kisses from Rache't. There was no guard to stop me from inhaling the sweet smell of her perfume. Making our way home to Lakewood we stopped to get something to eat. Later that evening, I went out with the family.

The first thing in the morning, I had to go and see my parole officer and get instruction from him. Now on parole, I couldn't get caught doing anything wrong, or I would be right back in prison. In fact, I still belonged to them as long as I was on parole.

I tried to figure out what I was going to do to make some money. My mom was always there to have my back no matter what, and as ignorant as it may seem, I still hung out drinking alcohol and smoking weed. Like many prisoners, after being released, we go right back to the vomit we left behind. There are various reasons for this, such as failures in the rehabilitation systems, in the government, and the family. But mainly it is because we did not have Christ. I will speak more on this.

"Most former convicts were rearrested shortly after getting out of prison: 30 percent within six months, 44 percent within a year, 59 percent within two years, and 67 percent by the end of three years."[5]

This is a shocking statistic for sure. As time went on, my feelings of hopelessness increased because I felt that society would never accept me because of the things I had done. I had a record, so no one would hire me, and I really didn't have any skills. I did have some customer service experience, but I was a convict at the bottom of the barrel. I was an outcast in this nation, and black. This was my frame of thinking, and I knew my peers felt the same way. We picked it up from the hood. I just couldn't see me having any worth to my kids or anybody else. If only I could provide for them. This, by no means, was my only struggle. Others attempted to go straight and do what people called "the right way," but most of them ran right into the same wall I did. With nobody to blame but myself, it was like I was in a prison worse than the one I just got out of. But this prison on the streets had more temptation. I found myself in a bad situation. I was stuck between two places: sit and do nothing for my kids or get some drugs to sell and start back robbing.

---

[5] Bureau of Justice Statistics, http://www.ojp.usdoj.gov/

Chapter Nine
MY OLD WAYS

I went on to buy an ounce of weed and turned that into several pounds of weed. Then I got some crystal meth and a thousand ecstasy pills. This got me into a world I didn't anticipate. I was dealing with a local organized biker gang, Mexicans, and blacks all at the same time. I was known for not trusting anyone, so it was hard going into the drug game. I looked over my shoulder all the time for people who might have been spying on me to rob me. This was funny because I was in the process of robbing a drug house myself. In LA, it was well known that your door could get kicked in at any time by the police or by rival drug dealers. It was best that you didn't talk about where you lived or what you did, even with the people in your own surroundings.

Selling drugs had become very hectic. The biker gang pressured me after I made the money to give it to them. They wanted me to keep selling for them. I got hooked up with them through a friend who was doing me a favor to help me get on my feet. He knew I could sell fast, in my hood and around Long Beach, the city I was now living in.

When I saw they weren't letting up on the pressure, I went to my hood and picked up some soldiers who I knew would shoot if they had to. When I arrived at the store the bikers owned, I went in to tell them to back off. I wanted to thank them for the help, and if I wanted to work with them in the future, then I would get in contact. They were known for being violent, and they didn't really do business with blacks. There was also the possibility that this third-party mid-level guy would have problems if his higher ups knew he was dealing to blacks. The meet went well, and I was on my way.

They got back to me and warned me not to sell anything in their town. That was okay with me because my hood was on the other side of town anyway. After a while, I got away from drug dealing because it brought too many risks, and I could do without the worry of going back to prison.

I landed a job at Stater Brothers grocery store in the meat department. I only got this job because I lied on my application. I loved it there, and all my co-workers in the store loved me. It made me feel like I was accomplishing something in my life. Maybe it was because I felt wanted by so many people. They didn't know me after hours, but I didn't care. I just wanted to fit in, and I was doing well at it. In fact, the store manager was talking to me about being a department manager in six months to a year. But when my ninety-day evaluation came back, I was exposed. They saw I had a record and had lied on my application. The manager was shocked and didn't want to let me go, but he had to. It looked like he felt bad for me, but I told him not to worry about me. Before I left, I let him know he was a good manager.

Rache't was both mad and sad, but she stayed by my side. I guess she saw something in me that wanted to do right by our son and my kids. From the beginning of our relationship, Rache't always called Tommie and Tommiya her kids or our kids, and I loved that about her. She approached our relationship with understanding and unconditional love.

My dad was always making a mountain of money in what he and his crew did. Eventually, I talked my way back in with him. I had no funds coming in except from a few robberies. The money went as quick as it came in. He had some jobs coming up where I would make a lot of money.

While waiting on this job to come, Rache't, Tylon, and I moved into our first apartment together in Banning, about twenty minutes away from Moreno Valley where my dad and her family lived. Banning was a small town in Riverside County and very quiet for a big-city boy like me. It was okay because I was a man taking care of his family. Tommie, Tommiya, and their mom, Antoinette, moved all the way to California City, a little desert city about an hour and a half from me. I spoke to them often and Antoinette was very good at bringing them to come see me. She was a good mother to them, but I felt like I was letting them down as a father with regards to providing for them. Sometimes, privately, I would cry because I wanted better for them; I wanted them to have the world. But with my record, it seemed impossible.

The time had come for me to make some money with my pops who didn't really want me to be doing what he did. But he understood it would be hard for me to support three kids on an eight-dollar-an-hour salary. So it began. My pockets were fat with cash, bills were paid, and food was on the table. The job was great, and I made a lot of money, about fifty thousand dollars. As ignorant as it may seem, we kept up our activities until our activities ended with an arrest.

ME AND DAD IN PRISON TOGETHER

My dad and I were arrested together. We landed in Banning County Jail, and then we were sent off to Riverside County Jail. We were in disbelief that we were in jail together. As we entered the cell, I made a young man give up his bottom bunk because my dad's back and health weren't so good. Awaiting court, we made the best of our time together, but as my dad, he felt guilty. In my eyes he wasn't at fault. It was my fault for putting him on a guilt trip to bring me on board. To pass the time, we played board games and cards all night and talked about how to win our case.

Then things became more interesting. A doctor was arrested and sent to our pod. This man was in terror. My pops assured him that we would protect him on one condition. The one condition was that he would be my dad's personal doctor while he was locked up. We didn't really make him be our doctor, but he did hook us up with a lawyer friend of his for letting him hang out with us.

The lawyer didn't really help us any because we were both on parole and had numerous other convictions for the same thing. We both got two-year sentences. While waiting a few months to be transferred back to the California Department of Corrections, we were sent to the Murrieta Jail, a part of the Riverside County Jail system. My dad and I were split up and on a twenty-three-hour-a-day lockdown. We came out one hour daily to take showers and watch TV. Racial tensions were very high with blacks and Hispanics having riots throughout the facility. This guard, who was a bodybuilder, would fight any inmate who called him out. Inmates would call him names and use known bodybuilding jokes. When they did, he would tell the watchtower to pop their cell door, and then he would get in their faces. Some inmates would strike the guard only to encounter a flurry of blows to their bodies. One inmate was able to do some harm to this monster, but not much. This was jailhouse fun for us.

I think this guard thought this would stop a riot from happening. Usually when a riot kicked off, every building had to fight, no matter what races were going at it. As our doors opened one evening, we were attacked. To my surprise, I witnessed stone-cold killers running from the fight because we were out numbered. One guy had the top of his bald head to his forehead slashed by a razor blade.

Because of the riot, we were now on a twenty-four-hour lockdown until we were transferred to Delano State Prison. My dad and I were separated again when we got to the prison, but we ended up on the same yard. Father and son with the same name. We were the talk of the prison.

GOLDEN STATE CORRECTIONAL FACILITY

Only during yard time did my pops and I have time to spend together. We were already over the fact that we were in prison together. After our time at Delano State Prison Reception Yard, we processed out to different mainline prisons. I was shipped out to Golden State Correctional Facility in McFarland, and my dad stayed at Delano on another yard.

When I got to Golden State Correctional, I was already used to the ropes and fell right into the mix of things. I started my workouts on the yard to deal with my stress. I was depressed, and I couldn't sleep for months. I didn't even want to watch TV because it hurt to look at things going on out there in the world. I was disgusted with myself and others around me, and the only thing that kept me from attacking someone or one of the guards was Rache't's letters. I would hear my name called for mail, and it was like light shining in the darkness of these prison walls. After a while, the light would fade away until the next letter came. I think this was the worst jail experience I ever had. It seemed like every prison I went to was on the brink of chaos. Racial tensions were so thick that I started to hate blacks and Hispanics. Grown men fighting over the TV time. And they were serious! One's respect was lost if he didn't defend the TV. If you showed any weakness, other races would capitalize from it.

I felt sick to the bone. My stomach always hurt, and I missed my kids. I thought of how much I had failed them. I was truly down on myself and rightly so, but I still couldn't understand what I had to do to get better. I saw jailhouse Christians walking around happy, but I thought it was all a front to deal with the fact that they were just scared to be locked up with killers and gangsters. That was their way of avoiding conflict. One Christian guy in particular was always so joyful, kind of like he wasn't even in prison. In each jail, there's a guy just like him. It's as though God put them there on purpose. It felt like this guy could see right through me when he talked to me. He saw I was disturbed and came over to talk to me. He invited me to Bible study. I could really sense that this guy was different, but I struggled with the fact that he could be this happy. In the back of my mind, I thought he was faking it. The investigation was on. It was at least something for me to do, so I went to Bible study.

For a few weeks, I listened but soon I became very out spoken, and started to point out the flaws regarding God, or so I thought. I lashed out at the very man who tried to help me. The others still tried to convince me of the truths of the Bible, but it was all BS to me.

I drew away from the Christian Bible study, but I always kept an eye on them. I couldn't figure out how these men were so sure of themselves that Jesus could save someone like me from the inside out. Besides, they were criminals like me. I thought, *I can't believe these convicts with their silly, emotional Bible meetings.*

I was stressed out because Rache't was not able to keep money on the phone for me to call. I was also frustrated at the ignorance of the prison politics. Because the blacks were outnumbered, we had pressure from both the white and Hispanic prisoners. We had to compromise our activities to give in to their demands. I didn't like that at all. I was already pushed to the limit. I was sick of everybody, but I couldn't let that be known because that kind of attitude could get you killed in there really quick. I already saw killings and rape in prison, and I wasn't going to be added to the menu that easy. Behind bars, anybody can become a victim if you come in there with the wrong attitude. Even if you're a stone-cold killer, you will have your day if you stick your chest out like you're running the show or think you're better then somebody else.

Chapter Ten
STANDOFF OVER THE TV

It finally happened—the standoff over a TV. Yes, a TV! Not drugs, not gang stuff, but a TV. The Hispanics (Southsiders) wanted more TV time because they felt cheated that the northern Hispanics and blacks would watch BET music videos all day. They felt we should be watching movies, but the blacks weren't having that. So we had a meeting out on the yard with blacks from all the other units to see if we were to attack first or if we would agree with them. Most wanted to keep things the same, which meant war. The guards, being aware of what was going on, had given us time to iron things out by ourselves. But when the tension thickened, the guards started taking us down and pulling out key players in the talk, including me. We were sent to solitary confinement (maximum lockup), and some of us were shipped to other prisons because of our track record in the prison system.

For months, I was locked down in a little box that was freezing cold for twenty-four hours a day. I was very depressed. All I could have was a Bible, but I didn't read it much. I just thought a lot about family and evil thoughts of suicide. While I was in the hole, I do remember one time saying to God, "If you're real, appear or send an angel to show that you are for real." That didn't happen. I did eventually read some of the Bible, but I couldn't understand most of what I was reading. My mom was also deeply on my mind. I thought of how much of an embarrassment I was to her and how I let her down. I felt like a nobody and that I was a mistake to have ever been born. I thought, *Just look at me in this box like an animal.* I also remembered all the racist things my friends and I would talk about, like how the white man put us there, the government was set up to keep the black man down, and the white man was the one who brought drugs to us. I believed that the white man had stolen our identity and turned us against each other. It seemed I would be stuck in a lockdown environment like this for the duration of my stay, and that is where I stayed until my release. It was a dreadful time, but I adapted like we all do after a while.

GOING HOME AGAIN

I was released once again from prison, and this time I felt like it would be the last time I would be going to anybody's jailhouse. Then again, I had heard many people say that over and over again. I also witnessed people get out and come right back to the very same prison and unit they had just left. You may wonder if people ever learn their lesson after being locked up. Truthfully, the world is its own little prison, filled with billions of people who are in rebellion to God, and they are in the exact same position as anyone who is locked up behind bars without God. I was in this same spiritual prison while I was in solitary, although I didn't really believe it at the time. The Bible says everyone has broken God's laws. We just got caught for some of our law breaking. Even still, I had trouble understanding the Bible.

The day after my release, I had to check in with my parole officer, and that went well. He assigned me to a company that helped prisoners get jobs. They had some ex-prisoners speak to us about changing our lives. I took a couple of leads, but did not get a job. So

I just hung around my mom's house because Rache't had lost the apartment when I went to prison.

Rache't's dad, Earl, had worked with Long Beach Hilton for many years and accepted a job offer in Las Vegas to work at one of their properties. Rache't wanted to move there to be close to her parents. Her big sister, Latasha, was moving as well, so Rache't asked if I would be willing to make the move. I thought this might be a good shot for me to get it together with a fresh start, a place where I didn't know anybody and they didn't know me. I put in a request to my parole officer for a transfer to another state.

LAS VEGAS DAYS

Making the move was fun. Rache't and I moved to an extended-stay unit until we found an apartment. My introduction to Las Vegas was interesting. On my first night there, I was outside drinking a beer in the car with the music playing, and the police pulled up right behind me. The officer walked up to the window and said, "Get out of the car and drink your beer." I said, "Yes sir. I'm sorry about that. Thank you, officer." I thought, *I love Las Vegas*. That was the nicest thing a cop had ever done for me.

Making phone calls to California, I found out that two guys I knew had moved to Las Vegas: Rab Deuce from Compton Piru and a friend of the family for many years and TK, a guy from Black P Stone Bloods who had been in prison with my father. In fact, TK was my father's right-hand man in prison, and he reminded my father of me. We were introduced over the phone before his release. When he got out, he was on my dad's crew and became part of the family. We hung out quite a bit.

TK moved just two days before I did. He knew a leasing agent who could get us an apartment. We moved to the northwest area of Las Vegas . . . in the hood.

I didn't even know Las Vegas had a ghetto. I figured it was the Strip and few surrounding communities and that's it. I was in for a surprise. Rache't, Tylon, and I got settled in to our new apartment. Even though we moved to a bad area, all I wanted was for Rache't and my son to be safe and happy, and I would do anything to keep it that way.

When I arrived in Las Vegas, I had the mindset of starting fresh, but the reality of having old friends there in Las Vegas with me clouded my thinking. Right away, I got back into the habit of hanging out. I did, however, manage to get a job at a call center. Unfortunately, it was crooked. It was full of people selling drugs at work. I saw another chance to make money, and I did. Criminals ran this place, and since I was a criminal, this gave me a big boost in the drug game I thought I had left behind.

TK soon got a job there, and we started on a journey to big money. Being from LA, we figured we had all the best connects on the West Coast.

Rab, TK, and I were like family. Rab had been in Vegas for a while, and so he knew the city well. This helped us with our operation. We made good money. TK bought a BMW, and I paid bills and took care of my three kids.

Rache't landed a job leasing apartments, which she still does today. With all the things I put her through, she never left me or turned her back on me. She supported me in all I did even though she didn't agree. We went on to have another beautiful son named Tyrus (TJ). We call him our Las Vegas kid.

In our new apartment complex, it was common for people to hang out until two or three in the morning playing loud music. They knew I had a newborn son because they would hang out on the stairs all day and see us coming and going. I got to know them a bit because it was the neighborly thing to do. I did not know that Las Vegas gangs really didn't like people from LA.

Chapter Eleven
TROUBLE IN SIN CITY

One day when we came home from a family shopping trip, there were about twenty guys hanging outside drunk and sitting on our stairs. I was carrying my newborn, TJ, in his car seat. These guys would not move to let us by. Grown men, as well as young gang members, were there. I got angry and I told them to part like the Red Sea. After a minute, they did, all while yelling threats. I really wanted to do something to them at this point, so I called up my friends, TK, Rab, and Kuffs. They brought with them ten more men. They made it to my house faster than the police to a homicide call. They came hopping out of their cars with guns ready to shoot at anything that moved. They took it personally because we were family. Before long, my neighbors and the other gang members called a peace treaty. This established with them that I wasn't a pushover.

Still, I felt like I was back in prison, so I stayed on alert. I was ready to fight with every little thing they did. I would put on my gloves, grab my forty-ounce and gun, and make threats to anyone who disrespected my house in any way. A few times after that, I had to pull my gun or flash my gun at people in my building for hanging out on my stairs making noise at night.

As people started to get to know me, I gained respect from the community, and I respected them back. Like me, the gangs in

Las Vegas were ready for anything, so I became friends with a few of them. One guy in particular was the coolest cat in Las Vegas. He was my boy Lee Mac from the G Park gang.

The money from my sales was slowing down, so I started back doing things I knew best—robbing people. In the middle of all of that, I got another job as a bouncer at a club in downtown Las Vegas. On some nights, this club was a hip-hop, R&B club, and on other nights, it was a comedy club and bar. I got a chance to meet celebrities and local artists who would perform at the club.

TROUBLE AT THE CLUB

At this club, we would have rap battles with local rap groups. The mix of gangs, drugs, rap, and out of towners turned out not to be a great combination. The club owner knew I was well respected and had a lot of friends who came to the club, so that put him at ease just a little bit. However, the groups of people who came in were out of control. They would smoke and drink outside the club because most were too broke to buy alcohol inside. So they brought drinks from the local store and got drunk before they went in. This meant the environment was just right for fights and shootings to take place. And they did!

On New Year's Eve, while I was on guard, a few rap groups performed. The first group had about fifteen guys on stage at one time, and they were all high and drunk. After they performed five songs, they wanted to keep going, so they went over to the DJ booth and asked for a few more songs. When the DJ's response was no, they got mad and start cursing him. A fellow guard came over to tell me what was happening. I told the group that was it; there would be no more songs because we had other groups. They proceeded to threaten me. I told them I would change into street clothes, they could get their biggest guy, and we could fight. They didn't know I had a bunch of homeboys in the building. I escorted them to the door. Once outside, things got heated and one of the younger guys ran to his car and got a gun. He came over pointing the gun at me from a distance. I told him, "Where I come from we shoot people in the face." So he shot at me six or seven times. He missed me, but he hit the club and the club owner's truck. I think with all the pressure and stress I had on me, I started to lose my mind more than ever before. I was getting worse. Death was nothing to me.

I began hunting for the guys who shot at me. I knew of some people who knew them, so I terrorized a few neighborhoods. About the time I found out where they lived, they had just moved out two days prior, and no one would give them up. I did not want it to come to this. I was just trying to work a straight job.

My family and I finally moved to East Las Vegas, where things were quieter. Although we were away from the routine shoot-outs of our previous neighborhood, I became more of an alcoholic and very disrespectful to Rache't in front of the kids. This would cause me to have to leave the house a lot and go hang out on the streets and hustle, rob, and steal. I was not only a severe alcoholic, but I continued to take pills and smoke weed. I was really losing it. I was a bitter jerk and lashed out at everyone. Even my friends would catch my wrath if they said or did the wrong thing, showed any sign of weakness, or touched my drink. I would feed on it. I had lost the club job, and even with Rache't working, we were set back in all our bills. The lights got turned off for the first time—it wouldn't be the last time. I was so depressed and sick of myself. I felt like I was nothing and of no value to anyone. I remember looking in the mail with the hopes of some secret money or an envelope sent to the wrong address with someone else's money or a credit card in it. I even looked on the street by cars a few times, hoping someone had dropped their wallet or money. I was a drunk and in a state of panic.

A DESPERATE TIME

I became more and more of a loose cannon. I started looking for ways to rob wealthy people in the city, anything to make some money. I had connections with underground businesses. With my experience as a bouncer, I got to know very wealthy people who needed things done. And I got them done.

Because of the respect I had from black gang members in town, these wealthy people would hire me from time to time. Slowly, I backed away from them because of some of the things I was getting into, but we parted on good terms.

All the while, Rache't and I started to grow further and further apart. I was never home, I had no steady job, and I was always drinking and high. In addition, I had stopped spending time with my kids. It was all about me, and she was getting tired of it. I went back and forth to LA to get away—run away—from my problems. I blamed everybody but myself. I denied I was a drunk. I denied everything. My family saw it and would tell me I was losing it, but I didn't listen.

I ended up in the hospital with a blood pressure of 220 over 110 from sixteen years of alcohol and drugs abuse. They kept me at St. Rose Dominican Hospital in Henderson, Nevada, for two weeks. My darkness stayed dark with a bitter hate for all people and all things. Suicidal thoughts rang through my mind like a voice was talking to me. One morning at 3:20 a.m., I sat up in bed and started to cry. I felt smothered and couldn't breathe. At that point, I would have done anything just to die. I couldn't look Rache't in the face. I was a no-good father to my kids, even though they loved me dearly.

ALCOHOL AND WIVES DON'T MIX

After my release from the hospital, I still would go at Rache't like a mad man. I punched holes in walls and smashed household items in anger, trying to scare her. Then one day we had it all out. We got in each other's face, and I pushed her away from me after she threw a lightbulb at my head. She called the cops, and I was on my way to jail. Oh man, the anger and hurt I felt. I never thought she would call the cops on me. See? It was still all about me. I still didn't think of her feelings until I hit the jail cell. Then all the memories of her standing right by my side through all the stuff I put her through came flooding back. What a jerk I was! When they let me out, I had to enroll in domestic violence classes.

Now, to TK, my new nickname was Lightbulb. Rache't was like a sister to him, and TK was like a brother to me. We became very tight through the years.

Robert (Tic Loc), who lived in my mom's neighborhood back in Cali, had also become like a brother to me. We had been friends since 1997. He knew my whole family. He was with my family more than I was because I moved and had kids. Rob looked after my mom and sisters Tanya and Tasha every day. His family is my family and vice versa.

Rob and his girl, Nicole, whom he would go on to marry later on, came out to visit us. We went out on the town drinking and gambling. We were just enjoying our time because we rarely saw each other. Now drunk and leaving the MGM Grand, we pulled on car door handles to see if any were open. One of the doors opened, and we searched the car. We found keys to the car and started to drive it. We got one block and the cops were on us. I swerved and hit a fire hydrant. I have no idea what possessed me to do that. We were just out having fun. Now, we were on our way to jail. I got booked and bailed out the next day, thanks to Rache't. I ended up getting probation because I didn't have a record in the state of Nevada, so I caught a break.

After this, I chilled out a bit, doing my best to avoid any more dumb activities. But what I didn't chill out on was my drinking. I started drinking a fifth of hard alcohol a day.

Chapter Twelve

SUICIDAL THOUGHTS

It felt like I was in a dreamlike reality where I couldn't really think clearly. My blood pressure was still high. My friends and family were scared of what I might do next. At home, I was a monster and antisocial. I didn't talk to Rache't much. I kept my distance from her because we always argued over everything; I was either drunk or high and always had to be right. A deep hate was brewing inside of me, a prison worse than any physical prison. I was trapped in this body of filth and evil. The memories of all the families I destroyed or hurt in some way and all the things I did seemed to torment me. I thought about all the hurtful things teachers, family, and friends ever said about me. It seemed like everybody hated me. I actually hoped that a blood vessel in my brain would blow from my high blood pressure, and I would be relieved from this pain. It was the first time I had suicidal thoughts.

Night after night, I couldn't sleep. Some nights I would only sleep an hour. I would waken with demonic nightmares and dreams of prison. Those nights turned into months as I stayed up with a knife by my side, thinking of how to take my life while my family slept. On the other hand, I thought about my kids not having me around and how much it would hurt them if I killed myself. I thought about how they would have to live with the memory of their dad committing suicide in the living room while they slept. It was those very thoughts that stopped me from going through with it.

Rache't had to ask her parents to help us out with the bills. My mom did what she could do as well. But I didn't like asking her for anything. In fact, I could count on my hand how many times I had asked my mom for anything. My dad had taught me to stand on my own two feet and get my own money.

It wasn't that easy for me to get money unless I took it from someone. One night as I sat up drinking in a dark room—the electricity had been turned off—I told Rache't I was going out to rob. I drove around the neighborhood and no one was out. It was a strange thing that no one was out on the busy streets of Charleston and Nellis Boulevard. As I drove up Nellis Boulevard, it was like I was crying on the inside but tears wouldn't come out. This strong feeling was telling me to kill myself because I was worthless. I looked up to see a church, so I pulled into the parking lot. With my gun in my lap, I thought about my run-ins with the Christians in prison. When I looked into the church, I saw a bunch of old folks in a Bible study. I just drove off and made my way home.

LAS VEGAS JAIL

When I got back home the family was asleep, and I sat up for a while before going to bed. The next morning I was awakened by a loud knock at the front door. At first, I thought it might have been Rache't just coming back because she forgot something on her way to work. Through the peephole, I could see it was a white male with a badge—my probation officer. He came to remind me that I was still on probation and hadn't reported for a month or so. When I told him I had been calling him, he got loud. The kids had already gotten out of bed and were in the living room. They watched in fear as the PO slammed me against the wall and handcuffed me, and for no apparent reason, he called for backup. Ten minutes later, five other POs showed up.

They let me call Rache't to come pick the kids up, and then I was on my way downtown. As I sat in booking, it felt like I had been in a long boxing match. I sat there while undercover cops brought in prostitutes by the dozen and drunk people fighting the police and each other. I was in complete disgust. I looked behind me to see my PO at the window getting some paper work. His assistant walked over to me and asked, "Why do you have a warrant?" I said, "You're the cop. You tell me. I didn't even know I had a warrant." My PO told me the warrant was for a crime I had committed three years prior. I had left blood at the crime scene of a burglary I committed. I must have gotten cut breaking into the place.

My heart dropped to my toes. My whole world crashed all around me. I couldn't eat, sleep, think, and my body was weak. I sank deeper and deeper into a depressed and suicidal state, even though I didn't let the jail nurse know. They ask you every time you go into jail if you're suicidal or want to hurt yourself. I did, but I didn't ever want anyone to know it, not even Rache't.

I was booked and sent upstairs to my chambers. It was full of all sorts of people—pimps, drug dealers, and even tourists. My court date was in a few days, and I wondered what they were going to do to me. I got appointed a public defender. A few days later, he called and told me the DA was offering me ten years. I said, "Yeah right. I'm not taking that deal in a million years."

ANTISOCIAL, SUICIDAL, AND DEPRESSED

My family was shocked. Rache't kept assuring me I was coming home. I was comforted until I hung up the phone, and then the reality of me being gone for a decade stung my soul. The only time my mind was clear was when I was playing cards or dominoes with other inmates. At lights out, the dread and torment would kick in.

After two weeks behind bars, the weight on my shoulders would not lift off of me but would increase. The walls seemed to cave in around me like they had a heartbeat. I wanted to go see a doctor because I was scared of myself. I needed to talk to someone desperately. Then one night I started to cry out, "If there is a God, you need to show up or do something!" Nothing happened so I fell asleep. I had a dream I was on a pier at the beach. A little boy walked over to me with his head down, and when he looked up at me with his deep red eyes, he grabbed both of my arms with his fingernails embedded into the flesh of my arms. He tugged at me, and I jostled left to right under his great power. I could sense he didn't want to let go.

Each night, the dreams became more and more strange. In the next dream, I was walking through a park and a man in all black was feeding the birds and cursing them at the same time. As I approached this man, I saw he was some kind of priest or preacher, and he was very ugly. As he fed the birds, he violently stuffed his face with food and said horrific things to me. I would come to find out later that all this attacking was demonic. Again, I asked for some angel or God to manifest. I was scared crazy.

The next day, I went to talk to this older black man I had seen when I first came in. He would sit by himself with his Bible, and I would go over and ask him questions from time to time. Other inmates would come to me and tell me he was a fake and a drug addict. But this man talked to me with confidence that one day I would get out and serve God. He was just so sure of it. I was overwhelmed at what he said. Even though my brain was in overdrive, what he said was so comforting. In a million years, I would have never thought I would be someone who would serve God.

Chapter Thirteen

A MIRACLE

That evening, a Bible study was called over the loud speaker. I couldn't just sit there. However, all around me, inmates watched me. Inmates who had gotten to know me from the streets and inmates I talked to every day. If I were to get up and go to this Bible study, it could be looked at as a sign of weakness and cause me problems I didn't need. But something was happening to me, and I couldn't control myself. I had to get up and go over to the church line with an "I don't care what people think" attitude. We walked in single file with our hands behind our backs to a room where the meeting was to take place.

When we got to the room, my mind started racing. I thought, *Why am I going to this meeting?* For the last few days, I had put in a request to speak with someone and no one would respond. I thought maybe these people would have something to say that would help me with all my stress.

Two tall, older guys—Tim Berends and Pastor Kleg Seth— stood at the front. On the table in front of them sat a boom box and a bunch of pamphlets. They were so happy and full of smiles. I could have said, "Bro, we're in jail and you're not, so stop smiling and being so happy. You're stressing me out with all that. We get it; you're better than us." On the other hand, it was somewhat refreshing to see the joy they had. I thought, *This will be interesting.*

The gray-haired pastor introduced himself in a very soft voice. "Hi, I'm Pastor Kleg Seth of Trinity Life Center here in Las Vegas." His assistant said, in a very deep voice, "I'm Tim Berends." Tim stood at about 6 feet 6 inches. He said he was a Christian radio host, and he passed out three hundred gospel tracts daily in the Las Vegas area, mainly on the Strip. He also traveled around the world handing out tracts.

They had us introduce ourselves one by one. I really was antisocial by this time so this was out of the box for me, but I went through with it anyway. We started by singing Christian music using lyrics they handed out. Some of the inmates sounded like they had been in church all their lives because they knew every song. After the singing, I realized I was having fun. After all, I was out of the unit.

Tim told us about his tract ministry and how God had led him to do it every day since the 1970s. He shared about his love for God and for us inmates. He also had a great sense of humor. He had us laughing as he told us some of the stories about people he encountered while out witnessing on the streets. Tim was a former corrections officer until he was let go for trying to give a tract to an inmate who was a practicing witch.

Pastor Kleg then went on to tell us that Jesus Christ was sent to die for all mankind and that included each of us. He proceeded to speak of a loving God who loved us so much He sent His Son, Jesus, to die on the cross for our sins. By doing that, all the sins of the world were forgiven and all we had to do was believe in the One whom had God sent, Jesus. He read John 3:16–17: "For God so love the world that He gave His only begotten Son, that whoever believes in Him should not perish but have everlasting life. For God did not send His Son into the world to condemn the world, but that the world through Him might be saved" (NKJV).

Pastor Kleg spoke about the apostle Paul and how he intensely persecuted Christians. Paul was in attendance at the murder of the first Christian martyr, Stephen. He spoke about how Jesus met Paul on the road to Damascus. Paul was converted and used in a mighty way. Pastor Kleg was using this passage to show us that no matter what we had done in the past, God can and will forgive us. There was hope. He explained that even if we were murderers, we would be forgiven. God loved us and was inviting us to accept Him and receive His forgiveness.

As I listened, I started shaking a bit, and my heart was full of fear, even though he spoke of forgiveness. I felt guilt. I felt filthy. Pastor Kleg told us we needed to repent of our sins, surrender our lives to God, and trust in His Son. As the meeting came to an end, I was stuck to my seat. I felt crushed, shaking, and I was breathing very deeply. I was trying to stay calm, but I was overcome with grief.

When Pastor Kleg said, "Everyone come up front, make a circle, and hold hands. Does anyone want to receive Christ into his life?" my hand went up and tears started to flow down my cheek. I prayed and at the same time cried like a baby. When the prayer ended, I went to Tim while Pastor Kleg spoke to the others. Tim prayed with me again, I became filled with God's Spirit, and had a burst of joy and comfort. I knew at that moment I was forgiven of everything I had ever done. I cried and cried as if to empty out all the trash I had in me. I was given a brand-new life. Words cannot express what was happening to me. I had joy I could not contain.

The guards came and the Bible study ended. As they took us back to our units, I went into mine a changed man. I had to tell someone what happened to me, and the first person I told was that little old man with his Bible. With a joy unspeakable I said, "Jesus is real and my life is changed, sir." He was thrilled and broke out in joy and praise. Amazingly, I had a boldness that even shocked me! I didn't care what people thought. All I wanted to do was tell everybody about Jesus Christ and what had happened to me. I started talking to skinheads, Bloods, Crips, and criminals from all walks of life.

I was in shock at my fearlessness in sharing the Gospel of truth to the men there. I couldn't put my Bible down. I would be up all night reading and praying. I prayed over the men as they slept. At night when the worries about my family would kick in, right away the Lord would settle in my heart that He was taking care of them.

However, one night, my worries got the best of me when I kept thinking that something bad was going to happen to Rache't and the kids as they drove to Rache't's family reunion in Arizona. I had just read the night before in the scriptures (Genesis 24:12–14, NKJV) how Isaac's servant went to Abraham's kinfolk's country to get Isaac a wife. He asked the Lord to let the woman who came to the well and said, "Drink, and I will also give your camels a drink" be the wife for Isaac. In my unit, there were two guards at the front booth just talking with each other. I prayed, "Lord, if Rache't is going to be okay, when the guards do their rounds, please let one of the guards ask me what I am reading." As soon as I finished that prayer, they started their rounds. When one of them got to me, he asked me what I was reading. I just stared at him. He asked me, "What's wrong?" I told him about my prayer. He stood there in awe. Then he said, "My wife and I are going to church tomorrow. Let me write your name down so we can pray for you." I cried because I knew, I knew, I knew God was there. He was really there with me!

The next day while lying on my back in my cell, I started looking at the air vents. Then I sat up and looked at the sinks and everything that was made. I had this overwhelming sense of God's presence right there, and I said to myself, "All this for us. How do You love us so much?" I laughed at myself because I saw God's love even in the air vents and sinks. I felt such great warmth and comfort that day.

The Lord had me start a Bible study. A little fear came in but the power of God overcame that quickly. At first, we had two or three, and then it grew to ten. I wasn't a Bible teacher; I just wanted to show people the truths that would give them hope and eternal life. I couldn't believe I was really doing this. Just a few weeks ago, I was antisocial and suicidal.

I finally got a chance to share with Rache't all that had happened. She was at a loss for words. I told her of the wonderful encounter with God and how He saved me. I proceeded to apologize to her for all I put her and the kids through. She said, "If this is true, then you're coming home." For some reason, she knew I was coming home, even with an offer of a ten-year sentence. I knew that the

Lord was speaking through her to comfort me in my worries about my family.

As the next week rolled around, I went back to Bible study on Tuesday, the day that Pastor Kleg and Tim came. This time, they brought two guys with them, Paul and Eddie. They each had a love for praying over the men. Paul showed a great deal of concern for the men to trust in God's healing promises. Eddie enjoyed sharing the message of redemption in Christ.

We had a joyful time in the Bible studies. One day, Pastor Kleg brought in his son, Nathanael. He was a tall young man who played guitar and sang. Although he was not allowed to bring his guitar into the jail, a thunderous voice came out of Nate as he sung praises to the Lord. It was an amazing sight. For Nate to be so young—nineteen at the time—and serving God was a shocker for me because most young men I knew his age were into drugs, gangs, and all kinds of illegal activity. I couldn't wait to tell my oldest son all that Christ had done for me, and I was even more anxious to tell him after seeing the wonderful work of God in Nate.

Chapter Fourteen
GOD WAS USING ME

As my Bible study grew, the Lord put it on my heart to ask the guards if we could use a storage room for our study and be able to pray away from all the noise. The room had a big glass window so they could monitor us at all times. To my amazement, they said yes and left a note to give the other shift a heads up on what we were doing. I had a Bible study in the morning and a big study at night. A couple of other Christians and I would invite all the inmates.

As I read chapter by chapter, I would give my understanding of the passage and everyone would comment and share other scriptures. I was shocked at how much everybody knew. The fellowship was a tight-knit group of guys who shared each other's burdens. Other inmates saw this and started asking questions. Some threw bitter insults, but that was okay because I understood the hate that was still polluting their hearts.

Men fighting various cases would come to me, yes me, for prayer before court. I started staying up at night, just waiting for anyone who needed prayer before they went to court. This added to our fellowship. I started leading people to the Lord, and others would recommit their lives to Christ. Some of the tougher inmates would pace back and forth past the storage room looking in, and some would just stare at us, secretly wanting to come in. So I would go out and tell them to come on in, and most would. When they came in, the Lord would deal with them in a mighty way, and soon this storage room was full of inmates who were singing and praising God. I still don't understand why God would use a wretch like me. Psalm 91, along with Isaiah 41:10, were the scriptures that truly blessed me during this time. "Fear thou not; for I am with thee: be not dismayed; for I am thy God: I will strengthen thee; yea, I will help thee; yea, I will uphold thee with the right hand of my righteousness" (Isaiah 41:10).

God is God, and His will and ways do not change. Most would say these guys are scared of doing their time so they get religious. Truthfully to this day, this is some of the best fellowship I have had. God deals with the lowest of the low in this way, away from all the drugs and temptations that had them in bondage. Know this: if anyone claims to have no sin, the Bible calls him a liar and the truth is not in him at all (1 John 1:8).

An inmate named Troy and I became very close. We would pray all night over our families, for every inmate in jail, and we prayed for revival. At least five times, Troy and I ended up reading the same scripture. We would pick a scripture each day that the Lord laid on our hearts and to our amazement, we would be on the exact same passage of scripture. This happened so much that we couldn't eat because we were so excited and full of the spirit. We started fasting once a week and fasting a meal daily. This was such a sweet time. Yes, we were in jail, but we had never felt freer.

With my court date arriving, I had a visit from my public defender, and she asked me what happened. I told her everything was true and I was guilty. However, when she typed up the report, she stated I was not remorseful. I believe she was wrong in saying that because in my heart it was settled; I was going to do my time and work the work of God while I was in prison. I didn't believe her report had any weight on the outcome of this case. In fact, I wrote the judge a letter stating I was sorry for what I had done.

A few weeks before I went to court, I posted verses from the book of Proverbs on a two-foot wall along the walk that led to the dining hall so that inmates could read it as they went to breakfast. Most of them would stop and read it. I wanted it to be a blessing and stir up their hearts and minds about the things of God. I also put up a prayer box for inmates to drop off their prayer requests. Many prayers were answered and lives were changed. I would go on to speak to inmates from eighteen to eighty years of age, and God would touch their lives. This was a miraculous time. I always wondered, *How could He use me, Tommie Scott?* Now I knew. I cried because of what God was doing. I was just in awe!

FACING TEN YEARS

The time had come for my court date, and I had an unexplainable calm in my heart. As I entered the court, a song came into my heart. I sang to myself, and tears of joy flowed. When it was my turn to speak, I said, "Your Honor, I want to apologize to the court, to the DA, and to the state of Nevada for what I have done." The judge asked the DA what they were going to offer, and the DA said the maximum of ten years. The judge looked down as if she were reading—I suspect she was reading the letter I had written to her—and she said, "I'm sentencing you to one year in the county jail." This meant I could stay in town instead of being shipped to the state prison. This also meant I could get out early for good behavior.

When I went back to my unit, everyone wanted to know what happened. They were all happy for me that I didn't get all that time because I had been there for them. They really wanted the best for me, as I did for them. Then an inmate who I had talked with—but who hadn't been in fellowship with us—told me I could apply for house arrest and that it would take a few weeks for a response. I applied and in two days they were calling my name for release. All the guys were shocked and amazed yet happy for me. Some were sad to see me go. I got a list of their names and phone numbers so I could keep in touch with them.

I was transported to a holding cell where they put a tracking bracelet on my left ankle, gave me my street clothes, and called for my ride. Rache't quickly arrived, smothering me with hugs and kisses. The smell of her sweet perfume was so welcoming. Now, I had such great respect for her. I saw her differently. The light I now saw her in was as God's precious creation, and her beauty was even more glorious.

TOUCHING LIVES ON THE OUTSIDE

Now back home, my concern right away was finding a church. I started attending the church Pastor Kleg worked with, Trinity Life Center. The head pastor there was Pastor Randy Greer, an ex-MLB player with a heart full of love for his flock. The church was very diverse with people from all walks of life—cops, ex-gang members, doctors, etc. You name it; they had it.

On Wednesday, I attended Bible study over at Tim's church, Four Seasons Fellowship. Their pastor was Bill Walker. A small group of folks met at a library, where they worshipped and had prayer. My focus was on winning souls for the King of kings. I couldn't stay away from that church. I would even attend the church staff prayer meetings. Being on house arrest, church was one of the few places I could be when I wasn't working. Places like churches or church services were okay because my house arrest officer seemed to let me do anything that was productive. I think he may have been a Christian or else God was just giving me major favor to move around and touch lives.

Pastor Kleg and Tim had me all over town sharing what the Lord had done. I went to nursing homes, churches, and all kinds of meetings. I couldn't contain the tears from flowing as I shared the wonderful work of God in my life. I was in the Word of God and praying every day. I would ask the Lord for a soul a day to minister to on the bus or the street. He answered that prayer.

A SPIRITUAL BATTLE

As a Christian, spiritual battles are a guarantee. Our apartment was directly across from the play area in our building and all day about twenty or thirty kids would be playing outside. One day, Tylon's bike was stolen, and a bunch of kids came and told us who did it. They even showed us where they lived. I went to the little thief's apartment and saw about ten people hanging around outside of their home, drinking and smoking weed. I told them that all the kids saw one of their kids steal my son's bike. The kid was only four years old. His dad admitted that his son stole the bike but that they already took the bike back to their house—this guy didn't live there; it was his sister's house—and that he would get it when he got a chance. I said okay and left it at that. A few days passed and still no bike.

A struggle arose in my spirit. I wanted so badly to call some people and force them to give me my son's bike. I called Tim and Pastor Kleg and told them what was going on and how I felt. A lot could happen, depending on how I responded. We had prayer, and then the pressure lifted. I went back to the apartment where the kid who took my son's bike lived. I told them they could just keep the bike, and I would be in prayer for them. I told them I would buy my son a brand-new bike, and I did. Tylon and I walked to Target, which was right behind our building, and got a new bike. On the way home, the only way to get to our house was to pass by their apartment again. They saw us and someone must have called the kid's father because he came over to my house with Tylon's old bike. I thanked him, gave him a hug, and I could tell at that moment that God had touched his heart. I let him know that I would keep him and his family in prayer. God is good. I was full of joy because I had power to do what was right and in doing so, a seed of love and righteousness was planted. Thank You, Lord!

Not being married wasn't a problem at first, but after a while, I really started to feel convicted. I needed to do something about it right away. Rache't and I had been talking about getting married for years, but at the time, I couldn't stay out of trouble.

I proposed to Rache't in front of her best friend, Kandyce, who she had known since grade school. After a few weeks, Rache't gave her life to Christ. At the end of a church service, an altar call was given, we went over to Pastor Kleg, and he prayed and led my soon-to-be wife to Christ. Tears flowed down her cheeks as the power of God touched her heart. God has been most gracious to us.

I had a talk with Pastor Kleg to start lining things up for our marriage. Soon Rache't and I had our first premarital counseling session, and we set a date for March 6, 2010.

Chapter Fifteen

THE BIG DAY

The man who married us was now a good friend of mine. Brother Louis was the head of Men's Ministry at Trinity Life Center and a homicide detective for Las Vegas. Wow! A cop was going to marry us. Doesn't God have a sense of humor?

I was cool all the way up to the day of the wedding, and then I got the cold sweats. I was so nervous! My buddy Robert (Tic Loc) and my dad tried their best to comfort me. I was so scared to stand in front of the large group of our family and friends. I had already been with Rache't for years, but I was still nervous.

Finally, my beautiful bride entered the building. I couldn't believe this day was here after the roller coaster I had put her through. She never gave up on me or lost hope in me. I knew this woman was heaven sent with a mission to capture my heart with her pure love and patience. And to think I almost threw it all away! The joy of seeing our sons in their tuxedos and my daughter in her beautiful dress was priceless. To the cheers of family and friends and with a kiss and dedication to our Lord, it was final. We were married!

One day as I was praying, the Lord put it upon my heart to enroll in school. As a convict, it would be difficult to get a job, but with academic certification, it would be easier. The medical field seemed to take too long, so I applied to High Tech Institute (now called Anthem Institute) for the Dental Assistant program and was accepted.

I was shocked, happy, and scared to be going back to school. My probation officer didn't seem to show much emotion, and the house arrest officer was very glad he wouldn't have to be chasing me down. They were both happy; I just know it.

My PO knew I had become a Christian, but he always looked at me with an eye of skepticism. I guess I was sort of a rare breed to him, and he wasn't sure if he could believe me. But I believe what he saw occurring in my life was slowly changing his doubts about me. He would tell me not to come in for a few months. I let him know I was praying for him and that no matter what he saw on the job with his clients, there was hope for each one of them whether he could see it or not. One day, my PO's partner told me to stand up and put my hands behind my back. He then told me he was only kidding, and we both laughed.

I had to take the bus to school an hour and a half each day because my wife needed the car. I was okay with that because I could see that God had major plans for these bus rides.

DIVINE APOINTMENTS

Every morning I would ask the Lord to give me opportunities to share the Good News with people, and He did. I handed out tracts and shared God's Word. Several times a week the Lord would set up a truly divine appointment with a lost soul who needed to hear from God right then, just like I did. The first encounter was right in front of my school.

I saw a lady who looked as if she had been at war. I could tell she had a rough life full of depression and hurt. The Holy Spirit moved me to go over and ask if she was okay. She looked at me as if to say, "Yeah right," and so I asked if I could be of any help. She replied, "Yeah, money or food." I had cookies from the school's mess hall in my bag. The next thing that came out of my mouth was, "Have you heard there is hope? Can I share with you what that hope is?" She said, "I have no hope. I'm dying of cancer, so what hope can I possibly have?" I replied, "You can have hope of eternal life. What is eighty years at the most compared to an eternity with God where every day is mind blowing because of how great and everlasting He is?" Then I proceeded to share that God sent His Son to die on our behalf and bore our sins on the cross. She repented of her sins right there on that street corner. I assured her that God had forgiven her. I also explained that all humanity is in rebellion against our Creator and that the world needed a Savior.

She wept and the people on the street looked at me as if I had done something wrong. But no one got out of his car. It was a simple proclamation of the truth, and I believe God worked in her heart deeply. I told her to find a church that was Christ centered and preached from the Bible. She agreed and we parted ways. Stand with me in prayer for that lady and her family.

In school, I became the Christian guy who always talked about the Bible and Christ. I had talks with a number of students in class and even with the teacher who was a Freemason from Texas. He was a very good teacher and listener. I spoke with a group of young partyers in my class who asked me a lot of questions, which I welcomed. All that did was make me dig deeper into God's Word. I gave them answers that caused them to question their disbelief.

I believe there are three main reasons why people reject Christianity: "1) *Ignorance.* John 7:40–43, where it talks about the misinformed, people who listen to things about Christianity and form an opinion from what other people say; 2) *Pride.* John 12:42–43, (a) pride in wanting to be approved by men keeps them from confessing Jesus as the Christ, (b) people just don't want to be ridiculed or suffer rejection for following Christ; 3) *Moral problem.* John 3:19–20, (a) some people reject the evidence because it means having to change their lifestyles, (b) they only accept the evidence that supports theories that allow them to continue their lifestyles, (c) some reject any evidence that may support a doctrine that would condemn their behavior and require a change."[6]

---

[6] Christian Apologetics, outline, "Why People Reject Christ," http://executableoutlines.com/ca/ca_01.htm

A GOD-GIVEN JOB

When I started school, I noticed I hadn't seen Mr. Johnson and his wife at Bible study recently. After about my fourth week of school, they returned. His wife noticed my scrubs and asked what I was studying in school. Her eyes lit up when I told her I was studying to become a dental assistant. She said, "My husband owns a dental lab." I had been fellowshipping with him for some time and didn't even know what he did for a living. My focus was strictly on God.

Mr. Johnson introduced me to the doctor he had been working with for twenty years. I started volunteering at the lab. After two weeks, I showed him that I could do the work and was a hard worker. Dr. Joe hired me while I was on house arrest, an ex-convict, and only a month and a week into school! I praised God so much that some nights it was hard to sleep because I couldn't believe what was going on. How was this all possible? The Lord says in Matthew 6:33: "But seek ye first the kingdom of God, and his righteousness; and all these things shall be added unto you." This is the absolute truth, my friends. All I cared about was serving God with the confidence that He promised to provide for all my needs as it says in Philippians 4:19–20: "But my God shall supply all your need according to his riches in glory by Christ Jesus. Now unto God and our Father be glory for ever and ever. Amen." The Lord will never let go of you. You may go through trials, but those trials are there to teach you the ways of the Lord. So don't grow weary in doing good (Galatians 6:9).

I worked hard in school, and my confidence had been boosted. I knew that I would have divine appointments while riding the bus, so even when I was offered a ride, I declined.

The next divine appointment I would have was on a bus that was packed. Usually I would have my Bible out reading, but it was just too packed and loud. I did manage to get a seat. It was like every man, young and old, was sitting down while the ladies were standing up. This was typical in Las Vegas. I tried my best to read, but a lady walked over to me and yelled for me to get up. She really tore into me. I got up. If I were not about the Lord's business this day, I would have missed out on what was really going on. When the seat next to her opened up, I purposely sat down next to her. I told her I agreed with her about the youth of our day and how there were hardly any gentlemen left. I probed a bit and found out that she was on the way to an AIDS clinic. She was not only dying of AIDS, but also dying without Christ. I shared the Good News with her and prayed with her until we pulled up at the hospital bus stop. She got off the bus with a new hope only found in Christ.

Day after day, the Lord would line me up with different folks—at-risk youth, drug addicts, college students, homeless, etc. In the early hours, get with God in prayer and read His Word. If you knew you could do something that would impact a life for an eternity, would you do it? Get alone with God in a private prayer closet and commune with your Lord. After all, you can go right to the throne of grace anytime, and God will give you the power to walk close with Him if you ask.

Let me share one story that really showed me that God could use any of you reading this book if you walk in the Spirit daily. On my way to the library, I caught the wrong bus. It went to a street that had no other buses running for another hour and a half. I had to walk for a few miles to another bus stop. When I got there, I saw a well-dressed man sitting there with his head down. He looked up a bit and then put his head back down. In a soft voice, he asked me what time the bus was coming. Then he said, "Can I tell you something? For some reason, I feel like I have to tell you this." He told me that his wife had died two weeks prior and he didn't want to live any longer. He was going home to commit suicide. Next to him sat five big bottles of very high-end vodka. I asked if his wife knew the Lord. Just as he said yes, the bus pulled up. On the bus, I reassured him his wife was in glory and suicide was not the answer. He knew the Gospel, but I shared what God had done through Christ anyway. The Gospel is the power of God. The simple Gospel will regenerate a person. He and I laughed and cried together. This was another divine appointment.

Going to a nursing home with Pastor Kleg and Tim twice a month was a blessing. Many of the elderly there had been nearly forgotten by their families. Others had a loving family, but because of their condition, the families could not take care of them. Pastor Kleg, Tim, and others from Trinity Life Center had been going there for years. On Christmas, we had the kids from the church come and sing to the patients. This was, and still is, such a blessing to see the elderly saved and on fire for the Lord, singing with shouts of praise. Being a part of this ministry has really been a heart-change experience for me, reminding me of how little time we have here on earth.

One of the ladies from our church who went with us to the nursing home was a ninety-two-year-old lady named Charlotte. Her daughter, Audrey, went with her. They were such a joy to be around. Charlotte's husband was an evangelist with the Church of the Nazarene and went home to be with the Lord some time ago. Charlotte was a fiery lady who had the zeal of a new convert. I'd never seen anyone so full of the Holy Spirit. She told me, "Tom, you're the younger version of a Christian, and I'm the older version of a Christian." She was saying that the fire that burns in us should be burning in the whole church, regardless of age.

After several months, I finally got off house arrest. I was then able to join Tim in spreading the Gospel through witnessing and passing out gospel tracts on the Las Vegas Strip and Fremont Street downtown. People cursed at us, called us names, and some would pull us to the side and ask questions in an attempt to debunk Christianity any way they could. In love, we were able to witness effectively. Bless Tim's heart. He was a sixty-seven-year-old man who had been on fire for God since the 70s, and he is still burning hot for the Lord today. Tim even went to Israel to pass out tracts with my good friend Mike. In addition, Tim has a Christian radio program called *Jesus and Tim* in Las Vegas on KKVV Christian radio. Tim is best known for his radio program out of Los Angeles and St. Louis, Missouri, called *Mornings with Tim and Al.* Tim is an angel to me.

Following the two men who led me to the Lord was a primary part of my continued growth in my walk with Christ. I watched, listened, and learned from these two men. They were bold, fearless, full of love, moved with compassion, and filled with the Spirit of God.

Dale Davidson and Guy Williams—owners of Keen 17, the only local Christian television station in Las Vegas—invited me to come on Dale's show and share what the Lord had done in my life. No matter how many times I share my testimony, I can never get through it without crying. In jail, I remember making a promise to the Lord verbally and in writing that I would never withhold my testimony no matter how nervous I was. When someone asked me to share, I wouldn't say I was busy. Dale and Guy are wonderful men of God who have given all they have for the sake of the Gospel. I think they are both examples of what being Christlike is all about.

Chapter Sixteen

MY FRIENDS' AND FAMILY'S RESPONSE TO MY CHANGE

My salvation has brought joy to my mom's heart. I can feel the joy in her voice and in her heart when I speak to her. She is so happy to know her son will have everlasting life with the Father. Currently, my mom is still seeking the things of God, so I continually pray for her. To me, she is so much more than an angel. She has been my refuge, a place of comfort and love. When I hated myself, her words would be my life raft and her love the calm waters.

By now, my dad had been in prison for three years and had five more to go. For the first time, to my knowledge, my dad attended a Bible study in prison because of prayer. My dad was so embedded in the street life we wondered if we would ever see the day my pops went to a Bible study. I continue to pray that the Lord will do a mighty work in his life and use my dad in a mighty way while he serves the rest of his time.

My sisters are very supportive of what God is doing in my life, and a few of them started going to church. The Lord is doing a work in my family, a family rooted deep in anger, hate, and violence. Most families where we grew up did not have Christ.

Many of my friends turned their backs on me for serving Christ. That's okay. I believe the Lord will lead them back to me one day. Some have surfaced and contacted me to see if what they heard was true. Some contacted me to seek counsel. Just as the Lord worked on me while I was in prison, He worked on my friends while they were in prison.

It was amazing to see how God arranged things to happen, perfectly and on time. Robert (Tic Loc) would prove to be the closest friend I ever had. Even to this day, he is a part of my family. We call each other brother. Robert is now married with two boys, and he is a manager at Target. Like many of my friends, Robert has been dealing with the fact that his conscience has no rest for the things we did. So he tries to drink it away, like we all did, to deal with reality. I'm proud of him for being a good father and working and taking care of his family. But without the Savior, Jesus Christ, his conscience will never rest, no matter how many good works he does. Jesus told Nicodemus in John 3:3, "Jesus answered and said unto him, Verily, verily, I say unto thee, Except a man be born again, he cannot see the kingdom of God."

"The phrase *born again* literally means 'born from above.' Nicodemus had a real need. He needed a change of his heart—a spiritual transformation. New birth, being born again, is an act of God whereby eternal life is imparted to the person who believes (2 Corinthians 5:17; Titus 3:5; 1 Peter 1:3; 1 John 2:29, 3:9, 4:7, 5:1–4, 18). John 1:12–13 indicates that *born again* also carries the idea 'to become children of God' through trust in the name of Jesus Christ."[7]

I have many friends who pulled away from the gangs, but they are still in bondage to sin, the lust of the flesh, and the pride of life. Unfortunately, without being born again of the Spirit of God, the misery will continue. This is not to say that we Christians don't struggle. We do, but what I'm saying is the Spirit of God confirms with our spirits that we are children of God. We can rest assured that if we repent of our sins and ask for forgiveness, He will forgive us and cleanse us. He gives us unexplained inner strength. He gives us

---

[7] Got Questions? "What does it mean to be a born-again Christian?" http://www.gotquestions.org/born-again.html#ixzz2QHsK9Jut

rest. He gives us peace and a blessed assurance that we will spend an eternity with Him. Romans 8:17 says, "And if children, then heirs; heirs of God, and joint-heirs with Christ; if so be that we suffer with him, that we may be also glorified together."

SPIRITUALLY BORN INTO A NEW LIFE

Apart from God, we are spiritually dead with no hope, no peace (in the storm), no joy (when facing trials), no love (for our enemies), and no eternal security. Without Christ, we have eternal separation from God in hell forever and ever. God, in all of His attributes, is in perfect balance. The justice of God says He must be a just Judge or He's a liar, and we know that's not true! Would a criminal fear a crooked judge who would let his crimes go unpunished? No! Would a just judge still be faithful and truly holy if this were the case? No. So the sins of the world must not go unpunished, or God ceases to be God at that very moment. So how could God be loving, merciful, and yet be wrathful and judge us all at the same time? How does God deal with the dilemma that millions struggle with when they say God is love, but leave out all the other equally perfect and true attributes? Romans 1:18 tells us, "For the wrath of God is revealed from heaven against all ungodliness and unrighteousness of men." John 3:16–17 tells us, "For God so loved the world, that he gave his only begotten Son, that whosoever believeth in him should not perish, but have everlasting life. For God sent not his Son into the world to condemn the world; but that the world through him might be saved."

How can both of these verses be true? Do we just ignore the wrath of God and cling to His love? Does God love man and hate man at the same time? If so, can we reconcile these two ideas? They reconcile at the cross. There, God's love *and* God's wrath meet and shake hands. The cross of Christ is a display of God's wrath toward sinners and His love for sinners. Jesus stands in our place, and God pours out His wrath on His Son in our place. God the Father does this so that He can pour out His divine love on us. C. J. Mahaney said, "Nothing else is of equal importance. The message of the cross is the Christian's hope, confidence, and assurance. Heaven will be spent marveling at the work of Christ, the God-Man who suffered in the place of us sinners."[8]

Eternal life is the gift, and you can have it now. Go to a quiet place away from everybody where you can pray and repent of your sins before God. Romans 3:23 says, "For all have sinned, and come short of the glory of God." You see, we all need forgiveness, the whole world does. Believe in the One that God has sent, His Son, Jesus the Christ. He bore the sins of the world on the cross so that you don't have to die in your sin, but you can be saved and have everlasting life. He rose again on the third day having defeated death and sin. What kind of love is this that God would love us this much? It's called agape love.

A few years ago, a seventeen-year-old girl in Somalia found some scriptures and while reading them, she got saved. She was born into the Muslim religion, and her family had severely beaten her for leaving Islam. At home, she was routinely shackled to a tree. "Her parents also took her to a doctor who prescribed medication for a 'mental illness,' he said. Alarmed by her determination to keep her faith, her parents decided she had gone crazy and forced her to take the prescribed medication." One source said, ". . . it had no effect in swaying her from her faith."[9]

While staring down the barrel of a gun, what can keep a little girl from renouncing her faith in Christ? Only the power of the Holy Spirit of God. This is only one story out of thousands about people who die for their faith. (The report is not clear on her cause of death, but her parents did beat her and drug her before she was murdered, in addition to trying to get her to renounce Christ.) This verse is so true: "For every one that doeth evil hateth the light, neither cometh to the

---

[8] C. J. Mahaney, Grace Quotes, "Jesus Christ–Death–Cross," http://www.thegracetabernacle.org/quotes/Jesus_Christ-Death-Cross.htm

[9] Posted on *The Christian Post* by Compass Direct News, December 4, 2010, http://www.christianpost.com/news/somali-teenage-girl-shot-to-death-for-embracing-christ-47932/#PevJeGER2puOjcRD.99

light, lest his deeds should be reproved" (John 3:20). John 15:18 says, "If the world hates you, you know that it hated Me before it hated you" (NKJV).

If you walk into a dark room, you will have trouble seeing. There are those who like the dark because they can do dirty, evil, and nasty things without other folks being able to see. Light exposes evil. You can rest assured those who live in the dark will try to put out your light. As they hated Jesus, so the world hates the light in the believer. No one can remove a single soul from the earth unless the Lord permits it.

I pray for revival in my family and friends, and I believe it will happen. South African pastor, teacher, and writer Andrew Murray believed God to save his family, and through his prayers, six hundred of his descendants came to the Lord.

Pastor Kleg's son, Nate, started a Friday-night prayer meeting, and about six of us have been meeting for several years now, praying fervently for our families, our city, and our country. The Christian walk is the walk of absolute surrender before God. It is a walk that says, "Lord, I want You in complete control of all aspects of my life, my family, my friends, my job, my country, and my soul." Trusting God is a perfect and sure trust, a trust that can't be found anywhere but in a perfect God whose Word never returns void.

"George Müller, a Christian evangelist and Director of the Ashley Down orphanage in Bristol, England, cared for 10,024 orphans in his life. He also established 117 schools, which offered Christian education to over 120,000 children, many of them orphans."[10] Müller trusted God to provide for all of his needs. "First, he never shared his need with anyone but God. Second, when he had a need, he opened his Bible, searched for a promise that fit that need, and then meditated on that scripture. Mueller believed in the power of thinking through scripture as much as he believed in the power of prayer. Third, he pleaded for that promise before God. And he didn't just pray for money, he prayed for individuals as well. Sometimes Mueller prayed for someone for as long as fifty years. He didn't stop

---

[10] George Müller, Wikipedia, http://en.wikipedia.org/wiki/George_M%C3%BCller

praying for anyone or anything until he got his request. That's how convinced he was that God would answer his prayers. Through his prayers, Mueller obtained the modern-day equivalent of $150 M for his charities; he led tens if not hundreds of thousands to the Lord, and he lived to be 93 years old. That was the power of his faith and life."[11]

I want the whole body of Christ to trust their Lord in this way. I challenge you to trust God to provide for you spiritually and physically. Are you lacking faith? The Bible says, "So then faith comes by hearing, and hearing by the word of God" (Romans 10:17, NKJV). Pray and believe and God will answer your prayer. If you lack love or joy, or if you are bitter, angry, violent, jealous, lustful, etc., just talk to your Lord and walk close to Him; He'll give you strength to overcome. Just look at Müller's life. When he had a need, he went right to the scriptures, found that promise, and stood on it. Brothers and Sisters, let's practice this together. Ask your brothers and sisters in Christ, "Are you standing on the promises of God?" If not, encourage them to trust and obey God. Let's give God the respect and glory He deserves.

FINISHING THE WORK

Along with Pastor Kleg, I help lead a basketball outreach program. I share with the kids what Jesus Christ has done in my life. I look forward weekly to being able to share God's truth with these kids and encourage them. The teenagers and young adults come from different parts of the Las Vegas Valley. We pray before every game, and it is exciting to see the Word of God transforming lives. Many of the kids are from low-income areas. We have guests come in and share powerful testimonies. We also warn them about drugs, alcohol, and the importance of committing their lives to Jesus Christ. We share the love of God with them, the love that Christ showed

---

[11] George Mueller, Man of Prayer, "The Greatest Man of Prayer of the Past Two Centuries," http://www.christianmanhood.net/reformers/George_Mueller.html

us. ". . . while we were yet sinners, Christ died for us" (Romans 5:8). Regardless of these kids' characters or what they have done or are doing we show them compassion. At the same time, we correct them so they can see the line of right and wrong more clearly. Some people wonder why kids from the ghetto act this way. Why do seven year olds overseas kill people with AK47s? Why do wealthy kids here in the United States who seem to have everything end up killing their parents or go on a shooting rampage? It's called spiritual warfare. The Bible says in 1 Corinthians 1:18, "For the message of the cross is foolishness to those who are perishing, but to us who are being saved it is the power of God" (NKJV).

> *Rock of Ages, cleft for me,*
> *Let me hide myself in Thee;*
> *Let the water and the blood,*
> *From Thy wounded side which flowed,*
> *Be of sin the double cure;*
> *Save from wrath and keep me pure.*
>
> *Not the labor of my hands*
> *Can fulfill Thy law's demands;*
> *Could my zeal no respite know,*
> *Could my tears forever flow,*
> *All for sin could not atone;*
> *Thou must save, and Thou alone.*
>
> *Nothing in my hand I bring,*
> *Simply to Thy cross I cling;*
> *Naked, come to Thee for dress;*
> *Helpless, look to Thee for grace;*
> *Foul, I to the fountain fly;*
> *Wash me, Savior, or I die.*

While I draw this fleeting breath,
While mine eyes shall close in death,
When I soar to worlds unknown,
See Thee on Thy judgment throne,
Rock of Ages, cleft for me,
Let me hide myself in Thee.[12]

---

[12] Hymn "Rock of Ages," words by Reverend Augustus M. Toplady, music by Thomas Hastings, 1763. Public domain.

AFTERWORD

I recently called my old elementary school to see if any of my teachers were still there. I wanted to apologize to them for giving them a hard time back then. Remember my grade school teacher Mr. Patton? The one who choked me? I found him! He is still teaching at the school. I not only got a chance to apologize to him, but I was able to share the Gospel with him. I found out that he had lost his wife and son, and being able to minister to him with God's Word was such a blessing. God is so good!

I am currently working with a local detective to locate the man I robbed and terrorized, who then invited me to have dinner with him and his family. I want to contact him, apologize for the robbery, and thank him for the kindness he extended to me in spite of my actions. I want him to know that even though I couldn't take him up on his dinner invitation, I was deeply affected by his kindness. I pray I find him well.

As for my dad, he has not yet received Jesus as his Lord and Savior. Yet. I continue to pray for my dad and his salvation. There is good news though. As of May 2013, he requested and received a Bible from my friend and mentor, Tim Berends.

As of April 2013, I joined the Southern Nevada Gang Task Force, and I am working toward becoming a licensed chaplain.

YOUR SALVATION

If you want to accept Jesus as your Lord and Savior and spend an eternity in heaven with Him, the Bible says you have to confess it with your mouth and believe it in your heart. Romans 10:9–10 says, "that if you confess with your mouth the Lord Jesus and believe in your heart that God has raised Him from the dead, you will be saved. For with the heart one believes unto righteousness, and with the mouth confession is made unto salvation" (NKJV).

I encourage you to: confess to God (out loud) that you are a sinner, repent of your sins, believe that Jesus died for you on the cross, and that God raised Him from the dead. Ask Jesus into your heart and to be your personal Lord and Savior. It will be the best thing you ever do!

More Inspirational Titles
from Innovopublishing.com

NEW.U by Jason Creech. Are you just getting started as a new Christian? Then you probably have a lot of questions. In this five-week devotional you'll discover a boatload of answers. Learn the simplicity of the Christian life. Welcome to freedom. Welcome to the new you.

ISBN 978-1-936076-64-2 , Paperback, $9.95
Available in eBook editions.

NAVIGATE by Jason Creech. For most of my Christian journey, I've searched for God's will. During the quest, I've faced confusion, anxiety, disappointment, and more trouble than I could ever have anticipated. But maybe I've had it all wrong. Maybe I don't have to search for God's will. Maybe God's will searches for me. Join me and over two dozen other pilgrims as we simplify the search for God's will. —Jason

ISBN 978-1-936076-67-3, Paperback, $9.95
Available in eBook editions.

BLINDERS, a novel by Kristy Shelton, portrays a beautiful relationship between a former slave couple, their love for a boy who wanders onto their farm, and the redeeming forgiveness of the heavenly Father.

ISBN 978-1-936076-65-9, Paperback, $12.95
ISBN 978-1-936076-74-1, Hardback, $19.95
Available in eBook editions.

More Inspirational Titles
from Innovopublishing.com

HOW GOD SANITIZED MY SOUL by Jonathan Okinaga. At one point I felt unlovable, hopeless, chaotic, and undeserving of anything good. The pain and despair nearly killed me. No drug, drink, meeting, woman, money, fame, or power could ever have fixed me—but Jesus did. This is my story.

ISBN 978-1-936076-14-7, Paperback, $12.99
Available in eBook editions.

A FOREST OF DOORS: AN ORPHAN'S QUEST by L. A. Muse. A young child, orphaned by addiction and isolated from her siblings, dreams of reuniting her family after decades of separation. She begins a quest and gains more than she ever dreamed possible along the way. A powerful true story of loss, love, spirituality, coping, and redemption.

ISBN 978-1-61314-167-0, Paperback, $12.95
ISBN 978-1-61314-166-3, Hardback, $19.95
Available in eBook editions.

WHAT MUST I DO TO BE SAVED? by James R. Anderson. This book takes us back to the Bible, in all its power, truth, and simplicity, to see just what God has to say about how to gain eternal life. You may be surprised at how simple, according to the Bible, salvation really is.

ISBN 978-1-936076-88-8, Paperback, $16.50
ISBN 978-1-936076-89-5, Hardback, $26.95
Available in eBook editions.

ABOUT INNOVO PUBLISHING LLC

Innovo Publishing LLC is a full-service Christian publishing company serving the Christian and wholesome markets. Innovo creates, distributes, and markets quality books, eBooks, audiobooks, music, and film through traditional and innovative publishing models and services. Innovo provides distribution, marketing, and automated order fulfillment through a network of thousands of physical and online wholesalers, retailers, bookstores, music stores, schools, and libraries worldwide. Innovo provides a unique combination of traditional publishing, co-publishing, and independent (self) publishing arrangements that allow authors, artists, and organizations to accomplish their personal, organizational, and philanthropic publishing goals. Visit Innovo Publishing's web site at www.innovopublishing.com or email Innovo at info@innovopublishing.com.

CPSIA information can be obtained at www.ICGtesting.com
Printed in the USA
BVOW07*1019181213

339139BV00001B/1/P